TABLE OF CONTENTS

Page

v

FOREWORD

"The Birches"

The "Birches" situated on Priorland Road, Dundalk was officially opened five years ago by Dermot Ahern TD. The dream of providing such a day care centre for persons suffering from Alzheimers disease became a reality on that very wonderful evening in June 2000.

Needless to say, much discussion preceded this event and many meetings were held by a dedicated and hard-working group of local men and women who saw that such a facility in our town was an urgent need. Massive fundraising was started and the North Eastern Health Board provided the plot on which the state of the art centre now stands.

Fundraising is on-going as the centre is only partially funded by the Department of Health supported by the North Eastern Health Board. The local North Louth branch of the Alzheimers Society of Ireland raises the balance which amounts to approximately 200,000 euro annually.

Our Dundalk Centre is a building of which we can be justly proud. It is built in an area surrounded by birch trees - hence the appropriate name. At the back there is a beautifully colourful enclosed garden where clients can enjoy the sunshine in a safe environment.

The Centre has excellent facilities and caters for 18 to 20 clients each day. The staff, comprising a highly qualified nurse manager and team of carers is most dedicated and hardworking. Their ultimate aim is to ensure that all are safe and feel welcome. The mood is one of relaxation and mellowness. The daily programme includes knitting, painting, reminiscence therapy, flower arranging, physical exercise, crosswords and the reading of the daily newspaper. There are also music sessions and sing-songs - all much enjoyed by the clients. Volunteers are also involved.

On arrival, (either by private transport or on the Birches minibus) the clients all receive breakfast. At midday, lunch - main course provided by nearby Louth County Hospital - is served and the day ends with a cuppa and some dainty teacakes at 3.15 pm. All birthdays are celebrated and special occasions are marked.

Our chaplain is Fr. Padraig Keenan, Adm Redeemer Parish. He is most attentive and a regular visitor to the Centre where he celebrates Mass on occasions. He and the choir of St. Nicholas' Church organise one of the highlights of the year - the Annual Christmas Carol Service for the clients and their families.

This is just a snapshot of what may occur in a day in the "Birches". Why not have a look at our website - www.thebirches.ie and see for yourselves.

Sr. Brenda,
Chairperson,
The Birches Alzheimers Day Care Centre,
Priorland,
Dublin Road,
Dundalk.

INTRODUCTION

New Poems of Oriel came into being due to a combination of reasons. A life-long love of poetry led to my working with poets as yet unpublished, and who were in need of some help in accessing information about competitions and other ways of bringing attention to their poetry.

The tradition of poetry writing goes back hundreds of years in the parts of Ireland formerly known as Oriel, Breffni and Meath. Much of the poetry formerly written in Gaelic has been faithfully transcribed and comes down to us recorded in articles easily accessible in *County Louth Archaeological Journals,* and other works cited below.

My own interest lay in the exciting period at the beginning of the eighteenth century when the style of poetry being written underwent an unprecedented change due to the fall of the great Irish and Anglo-Irish houses. The years of training which had been undertaken in the classical schools producing poetry were no longer possible. A new kind of poetry began to emerge which was later to re-emerge in the work of Patrick Kavanagh. This movement is significant, for it shows that in an absence of formal training the poetic impulse will burst a road.

> *"Almost in the twinkling of an eye Irish poetry completely changed its form and complexion, and from being, as it were, so bound up and swathed up with rules that none who had not spent years over its technicalities could move about it with vigour; its spirit suddenly burst forth in all the freedom of the elements, and clothed itself, so to speak, in the colours of the rainbow. Now, indeed, for the first*

time, poetry became the handmaid of the many, not the mistress of the few; and through every nook and corner of the island the populace, neglecting all bardic training, burst forth into the most passionate song"

County Louth Archaeological Journal
Vol I (1) 1904 p. 55

These are some of the reasons that led to my desire to find out what was happening outside the universities; in the schools, in the homes or workplace, on the road and anywhere else where poetry was been written. The result is *New Poems of Oriel*, a poetry book of the people. I sought submissions, organised a poetry competition, and from various other sources managed to collect what I consider to be quite a representative collection.

It became clear that there are many different kinds of poetic work. The people I worked with were writing poetry of vision that showed an intuitive understanding of the universe, of life, and the complex nature of humanity. I was in awe at the words that flowed almost effortlessly from their computers, in some cases like the celebrated "stream of consciousness". In most cases these poets had never been given recognition for the extent of their gift. Yet at the same time, theirs were voices that I believed needed to be heard, perhaps never more urgently than in the world today. I felt humbled and privileged that these poets trusted me and were willing to let me help them get recognition for their art.

Others, while not in the same category, were writing poems with perhaps a more widespread appeal. Some were comic, others tragic, at times deeply personal, and at times universal in their span.

Then there were those who executed their poems with exquisite craftsmanship. I have the highest regard for the originality of image and facility with words in these poems, which is truly admirable. There are many examples of this fine type of work in the book.

Subject matter in *New Poems of Oriel* is as diverse as might be expected from such an unusual assembly of people. Our poets range in age from ten to ninety! They include teachers, farmers, two childcare workers, a shoe salesperson, a librarian, mothers, fathers, administrators, factory workers, a hairdresser, a bar manager, unemployed people, disabled people, students, several children, a newspaper editor, a geologist, a shopkeeper, two priests and even a film actor.

It was a great boost to the collection when well-known and acclaimed poets Susan Connolly, Paul Perry, Gerry Corr, Vona Groarke, Conor O'Callaghan, Patrick Boyle, Bernadette Martin and Brendan Connolly agreed to submit some of their work. These are people whose poetry had already been published. The inclusion of some of their poems helped to bring about an immediate rise in the standard of the collection, in the eyes of those not yet published.

But what makes a good poem or even a poem at all? And how does one decide what should be included in any collection? *New Poems of Oriel* is not, and does not aspire to be a work of scholarly or literary merit. In compiling and making this selection there were two criteria. To what extent these have been met, the reader will decide.

In the first place, it was desirable that the collection be as representative as possible of what is being written in what was known originally as the Kingdom of Oriel. Opinions vary as to where the boundaries of Oriel are, or were. Broadly speaking the boundaries included what is now north Louth, south Armagh, parts of Down and Monaghan and extended to part of Meath. As already noted, the tradition of poetry in this part of Ireland is legendary. For those who have an interest in the subject, I can offer no better suggestion than that they procure a copy of Pádraigín Ní Uallacháin's excellent work: *A Hidden Ulster: People, Songs and Traditions of Oriel.*

Secondly, it was felt that to preserve the integrity of the collection in *New Poems of Oriel* some link with the ancient poets was desirable. An authentic voice needed to be heard. The links proved to exist mainly in the subject matter of the poems, but interestingly, some of the new poets have surnames that echo back to those of the older poets of Oriel.

The subject matter of the poetry in *New Poems of Oriel* plumbs the depths and scales the heights of human experience. The reader will encounter poems of love and hate, despair, anger, loneliness and all the great themes of literature. Tragic events from the domestic to the truly global, and events played out on the world stage are commemorated. Many poems depict a love of nature and homeland, adventure, childhood, nostalgia for times past, love of God and the spiritual world, historic and even pre-historic life in Ireland.

Perhaps it is a quintessential sense of Irishness which best defines this collection. It is a quality difficult to explain, but it might perhaps be what caused a late nineteenth century writer to exclaim:

> *"In England, the situation is often serious but never hopeless; in Ireland it is often hopeless but never serious".*

It seems to me that much of what might be considered mere verse in the elitist world of literature has a valid and indeed a historical place of its own, for no better reason than that many people identify with it.

Poetry books rarely become best sellers. Most of the general reading public admit that poetry does not interest them, they find it difficult, and sometimes confess that it is not worth the effort.

It is my hope that in the case of *New Poems of Oriel*, all who pick it up will find something to captivate them.

Mary Kearns
Dundalk
2005

FURTHER READING:

A Hidden Ulster: People, Songs and Traditions of Oriel Ní Uallacháin, Pádraigín, Four Courts Press, Dublin 2004.

Poems from the Irish, Neeson, Eoin, The Mercier Press, 1966

County Louth Archaeological Journals:
Vol I 1 1904 p 54–5
Vol I 3 1916 p 78-79
Vol III 2 1913 p 181-188
Vol III 4 1915 p288 and p318–322
Vol IV 1 1916 p 42–60
Vol IX 2 1938 p 115–123

About A Childhood

She haunts me in her love,
In folding faces of old women,
In crushed flesh on a gnarled hand,
In the tight clasp of recognition.

We shared a simpleness, an our-ness,
The mentality of the open door,
I was the son she never had
And she made me man o'the house.

An angel appeared in the oats-house;
Elizabeth lived up the hill;
Gethsemane was the boothery rock,
And I sprayed spuds in Eden.

Ellis Island crossed our paths –
If only I could tell her.
Going through the tunnel he'd 'sandhogged'
I felt soaked in transience.

Michael Murtagh

1

Addendum

It's there!
On your shoulder!
But you cannot see,
that 'THING' is nameless
but is there constantly.
It never needs rest
nor water
nor food.
It's colourless
nameless,
thrives on evil,
not good.

It doesn't have feelings
but moves into yours -
feeding your mind,
making you blind,
hands grasping
and grabbing -
"I want that!
It's mine!"

When people are kind,
it blanks out the good.
Suspicions abound –
"What's in it for them?
They must want something,
They can't possibly help!
They want something I've got".
hammers inside your head.

Feeding on feelings,
arresting the truth -
are you so blind?
See - you will find
the path to prosperity
is never lined

with loneliness,
avarice,
places you've been -
it's that 'THING' on your shoulder
that distorts the scene!

Now they're left standing,
so to hell with their lot!
You've had the last laugh?
Do they see what you've got?
You've had to cross rivers
to get to your goal,
swing from heights,
stand on stones
that moved eerily slow.
You didn't see hands
that guided you through.
Anything you've now got -
it's thanks to you?

And now you're arrived!
Where you wanted to be!
At the top of the ladder -
where all others can see
what a wonder you are!
How successful your life!
Your 'friends' buy you drinks,
to hell with the strife
that brought you this far!
Crooked wheels,
shady deals,
hands shaken in bars.

And there, on your shoulder,
It's that 'THING' you thank!
It's grown up now, you know,
it's turned into a plank -
made up of the chips
that got to your heart,

and hardened the softness
that once was a part
of your Life -
when you smiled
and laughed at a joke.
But know that side's gone
and you are left -
Broke.

Verna Keogh

Adventure

Caught in the room of self
Pleasure the ceiling, the floor is grief.
I reached and touched it
And have fallen hard.   It presses into me.
Does the strength of feeling push it further
Or is the soul's limit so defined
That others have the power
To so define?

Listen
I will make you large
What you thought walls
Become space
What you thought ceiling
Is sky
And the ground of your soul
I will lift up

Walk out into the uncreated
With me.

Mary Lisetta

And Love Forgives All

(For Jack Lawlor)

Way beyond our crude instruments
Of pleasure and desire,
Beyond all maps of understanding and
The stars we steer and navigate by
So far away...yet I know You're there.

Where the oceans thirst for sky,
Where the body disintegrates into soul,
Where joy kisses the brow of sorrow
And hate embraces love
And love forgives all,

Where guilt....is no longer guilty,
Just a crystal falling stream and
Pain and loneliness don't exist
So far away...yet I know You're there
Where spirits attract and mingle

In love's magnetism of the hidden
Holy Cosmos...somewhere...that somewhere
We're yearning to reach
On our way to...**'The Supreme'**
So far away....so far away....

Patrick Boyle

Angels

My karma visited me one day
Made me pay back my debts – and how I paid
I paid and continued to pay.

What I got in return was,
That feeling of rotting inside –
The green apple spiked by the worm.
It started to work its way into my centre,
It bored and split and left this searing pain
like a burning poker,
lodged in the solar plexus.
And it remained there.

I became accustomed to the routine –
unsettled, uncomfortable, unhappy,
But I lived until it started to fade –
When angels started to operate.

Time, hope, continuance and courage danced,
and waited until the angry flames died,
when sweet, warm daylight rose its rays.

Calm, settled and still,
Silent and cured of my ill.

Yvonne Kelly

Angels

(In memory of the dead of Beslan, September 2004)

The candles burn, and shine on the face
Of the brother in black;
He is the brother of the man who died in his arms.
In the darkness, young and old join together
In the mournful song - remember me...
I've wept for these candles - 340
Angels.
Angels gazing up to something we can't see,
Gilt in gold,
The candles they hold, white beads
Falling, rolling along the shafts -
I've never seen anything that look so much like tears.
Maybe it's the wavering light.
Light.
Semi-darkness, red glow from the 340
On the face of the Angels, Devil red
In the House of God.
Ghostly, the white glow on the faces, respected
woman...
Each one of them angels,
Archangels. Dark Angels.

Kathryn Lambe

Arsenal of Forked Tongues,
Say it With WMD

Ivory tower
Suspended
Above the

Common dust
Of Humanity

Pol Pot
Gadaffi
Ceausescu
Saddam
Bush!

Your oil is mine
Your state is mine
Your kids are mine
Your world.....
Is Mine!

Say it with WMD
Rocket launchers
Smart Bombs
Precision Targets and
An arsenal of forked tongues

Might is right
Smoke 'em out
Give 'em freedom
We'll say it with WMD
And an arsenal of forked tongues.

Bernadette Martin

Autumn Stakes Her Claim

Autumn stakes her claim,
Glazed skies take turn
Chased by the first crusted shade
Of an unsung season.
Days for fire and calm return,
Smoke stories...
And the gentle dream.
A wallow in what was
And what will be,
The sure ship's keel
That edges us past yesterday.
Province of dreams
And hushed promise
Breath-fog mornings
And wordless evening walks

Brian Eardley

Beautiful Flower

Early morning skulking awake,
slow eyes of dew crack open
and the sun hovers low in the sky.
Flower blossoms breathe life,
tilting petals soft, coloured
and joyous with open arms.
I come along buzz-buzzing,
skirking, waiting, hiding almost
until the time is right to pounce and prey.
But that song of love, oohh!,
calls me to her
and oh, beautiful flower of soul.
Ushering me to come and love her,
sweet nectar within
and oohh how I make sweet love to her.
Noble shades of purple,
bespeckled spots of bright yellow beauty
and anther of fertility.
Hours past yielding,
passionate tidings of conquering love
and careening feelings melt in the sun.
Time for my sad sad departure,
returning to my hive, my home
and 'til the morrow gently sweeps
the dark of night away away,
I will rest and rejoice
and love you once more.

Adrian Neasy

Beauty is in the Eye of the Beholder

What I see in you is a puzzle.
It – is – mysterious.
Why?
I am drawn to the whole idea of what you are
and the shape you choose to use.
The perception of a globe of air I hold in the open
heart of my hands,
trying to pick apart and figure out,
what you are.
and what it is that creates the most universal feeling in
the world.

Yvonne Kelly

Bitter Cup

On a surreal tv screen
the coffee lady
sips comfortably
while out of camera angle
people nameless as prisoners.

Live and die
bound to a treadmill
stumbling on a narrow track
from dawn to dusk
their hearts and souls hidden.

The fight gone out of them
as multinationals fleece them
just to give us a bitter cup.

Thomas Clarke

Black

My rose is black,
Why not red?
My blood is black,
Why not red?
My tears are black.
Where has the water gone that rolls down my face?
Why do I feel black?... because there is no light.
I hide away in a black room, where has the light gone
That comes in the door?
Where has the bright moon gone that shines in the
Window?
And the silver stars that shine with the street lights?
Why has the mirror gone black?
Where have I gone?

Where has the warm sun gone?
It's so cold, why is it so black?
Because I make it black, because that's how you feel...
Black.
WHY?
Because I don't let the light in to see where I go.
To be happy inside this world that I have come in to.
I can't get out.
It's like a graveyard... when you die, you don't come
Back.
It's like a wall holding you back.
WHY?
Please.... Just tell me why I feel black?
WHY??????

Leanne Quinn

Blackrock

Roaring sea upon the shore
Breaking waves against the bank
Foam flecked grey with power unseen
Eternal mystery deep within.
Change, unchanging,
Always there
Hidden danger
Not to care.
Deep mysterious depths
Terror in my heart
To sink beneath the waves
To know that we could part.

The calmness of the ocean
The deepness of the sea
Against the far horizon
As far as one can see
Sunlight shining on the water
Ripples on the sea
Sparkling, meaning nothing
Like my life to me.

Daphne Vernon

Body of the Sea

Rush to the shore my friend and hurry
Into the loving arms of the sand
Which embrace you and let you go never insisting you
stay.
The sun rays keep you warm
The moon beams freeze you in time
Until morning brings hope of a new day.
Many have treaded your waters in hopeful anticipation
and have been sucked in by your power.
You watch people dance on the beach, your eyes weary
and old.
You cover most of the world, not a place you haven't
Seen, yet they call you the virgin sea with hints of
pureness and romance.
Innocent you are not, no-one or nothing could know
more.
You keep it silent locked deep beneath the shore.

Caroline McEvoy

Border Lines

As I ride through the forest, leaves falling all round,
The clicking of hooves becomes the only sound
Of an age-old tradition, still living in our minds,
As once all lands were joined with men of different
kinds.

As I turn the dusty corner, sun peeping through the
trees,
I see a coloured man resting on his knees.
He stands up tall to greet me, we walk on, side by
side;
The orange sun is falling, he looks ahead in pride.
The dust turns into tarmac,
Hard-shouldered in with red,
A poppy standing in a line,
Remembering the dead.

Eugenia Thompson

Born

A rainbow of colour flashed in front of eyes
A film of sweat sparkled on my brow like a starry night

My heart pounded like drums of great warriors
Fireworks exploded in my head
I gasped and panted, filled with dread
Then you my beautiful baby were born!

Annette Donnelly

Breath

See here. The dust that beaded the inside of your
cheek
falls still on these letters, on the pages of a book

where someone else's hand will scuff its sleek veneer
and set it skywards, like seagulls astir

on the estuary, cheers from the pitch,
sleet from the Cooleys blown that way, and this.

Look up. Winter skeets the thin skin of the dome
and even the clouds condense the moment

into the here and now of your high mouth,
this flurry of words, or the thought

of what becomes you, what you might yet create.
So yes, let it happen. Let it be you. Breathe.

Vona Groarke

Brigit

(For Alison Kelly)

Run, little fox,
past hermit cell
and derelict castle,
past river and monastery
and quaint rose cottage.
Through oak wooded
centuries
weaving your way -
run swiftly now
in the open air.

Brigit called a wild fox
out of the forest.
That fox was you!
You played for a while
and went safe
through the forest,
the king on his horse
after you.

Brigit hung her wet robe
to dry on a ray of sun.
If they touched
her shadow
the sick were healed.
'Every stranger is Christ',
she said, and gave
to everyone.

People came to visit her.
A playful fox drew near.
She believed in mercy.
In the doorway of her
mother's house at sunrise
Brigit was born.
A fox howled

the day she died.
Brigit -
we name our daughters
after you,
Brigit, Breege, Breda.
After our mothers, sisters
friends
we call our daughters
Bríd, Bridie, Biddy.

Daylight will be cold
if your name fades
from our lips,
like a fire gone out
forever.

At the edge of Cuan wood
the fox goes,
no king of Leinster with him now,
though the same land
stretches away.

Brigit -
bright stillness in the sky
while I live stormily
below -

bright spark within.

Brigit búadach
Bethad beo *

Susan Connolly

*Victorious Brigit,
The living one of life.*

Brigit of Focherd;
Her Word From The Heart

I am Brigit- of -Focherd! I dance in The Gap-of-the
North!
Not a warrior or Brigand, but Dancer-of-Earth's Joy!
Crouch at my Holy Well, on Focherd, Hill-of-Breath!
Walk my Holy Stream, at Focherd, Path-of-Redress!

I Brigit, protect and nourish your Families & Flocks!
I Brigit, encourage Reconciliation!
I Brigit, inspire Healers & Artists & Poets!
I Brigit, Presence-amongst You-of-Mother Wisdom!

Lamentable indeed the serious Neglect-of-Me!
Remind your local church, Earth's Dancer awaits!
Not for Myself I bring this Strenuous Word!
But more than everything, for Her who Loves-All The
Folk!
I am Brigit-of-Focherd! I offer The Wisdom-you-
Lack...

Tom Hamill

22

Bullet-Points

Holstered up in darkness,
padded and shielded from breathing,
refined and special
and lost in holes of life
dug out of fake earth.
I am another dead child,
better off stillborn than being rejected
by the womb of each heart you touch.
The gun, so shiny, blinds my poor perfection.
You load me, remove me of my safety
and crash my life through perfect, harmonious,
mechanised, material glass.

The blanket darkness I once loved
has been removed, and as I move
naked and innocent, still flying,
I hear the drums of war pounding,
the bad water pollutants eating our blood.
Vomit stained grass and neglected skies,
dirty farmers raise aliens of sick.
Passing each barrier of strife, the
pattern of never ending ill lick
wounds of blood pus and AIDS
by the self interested Adam Smiths
of non profit, but money is all I see.
Counterfeited dreams of prosperity and hope
ripped out never-ending lives
and I spit and I swipe and
cry mercy to leave alone our earth,
but my flailing arms in vain
I toss,
So just die by my mother's side
in loss.

Adrian Neasy

23

Burning Down The Rest House
"My heart is not glad"

Where is the place of deep rest to be found?
Inside the whirlwind of the heart's turmoils,
where is the home of true peace?

When trouble fills all the hidden places
within one's breath-body-being,
how does one discern what is a true teaching?

When the spirit of mysterious love
calls you away from all that is comforting and familiar,
where does this courage to not know come from?

Who at the depth of dreams and coincidence
is shaping me into a new vessel
capable of holding more that is beautiful and joyous?

Who when my heart is not glad
is still singing to me from a source
that is older than anything or anyone in this life?

When resentment and self-pity still entangle me
with resistance to bearing the heat of initiation,
what angel is breathing mercy into my opening heart?

Kalichi

By The Light of the Moon

On a bed of pure crisp white
So high above the soothing lullaby of the sea
You're deep in peaceful sleep.
The clearest stars shine down just for you.
Their brilliance paint the darkest skies metallic white
Moonbeams calmly pour through your window and
Softly stream across you
Gently illuminating your beautiful face.
A silver blanket envelopes you
Embracing you, protecting you.
I hold your hand and gaze at you
Enraptured by such serenity
Such perfect silence.
My prayer for you whispers on summer winds
It dances through long silver grasses
Ripples through the quiet waters of time.
Listen, it breathes to remind you that
I watch over you for eternity
Every single night
By the light of the moon.

Lynn Dowling

Can She See Me Now?

White lights, bright and shining,
My street lit up, opened.
Down, down 'til the end
Can she see me now?

I shuddered, I shook,
I suddenly stopped dying,
Again and again 'til my remains,
Still in her presence and
I no longer feel....

Feel her, all gone and forgotten.
Verboten, verboten.
Whispers so soft to myself
Only my soul can hear.
Whiteness of my purity is
Tinted red, opened heart.

The birds I send are one by one.
Flying slowly up and up,
Floating in the air,
No longer the thane of corrup-t
Night turning day, not one row.
Shining bright, happy and at home,
I wonder can she see me now.

Adrian Neasy

Celebration of Drogheda

The Boyne God rises from the river,
the name 'Drogheda' firmly
on his drenched brown lips.
The hands of history envelop this town,
and it's geographical features
run to the sea.

Urban landscapes intertwine
with the Boyne Valley,
and Today and Yesterday
are embattled Kingdoms,
ghosts embrace the Chinese man,
as Drogheda explodes in
kaleidoscope colour.

Jacqueline Bannon

Christmas

Through the voices of children
angels sing
joyous bells ring
happiness in everything.

Candles are lit
with a ritual touch
from embers of yesteryear
holiness is near.

The solstice
with its new light
blesses the dawn
Christ is reborn.

Houses are decked out
with sprigs, spring green
to be pondered
to be seen.

Prayers said
for the living, for the dead
scriptures read.

Christmas is here
holiness is near.

Thomas Clarke

Cill In Cuile

The years gone by crowd round us in the graveyard of
Killincool.
The dead rest in tranquillity.
Early spring dawns with promising times, we're blest.
Where Laurence Crawley fought for tenants' rights to
rise
And Vere Foster helped educate the children in
wretched times.
Westward winds wind their way through.
Dreaming of continuing love,
Archbishop Michael Kieran championed men's noble
cause,
Enamoured with the poor.
Swirl around and see if I can. The Bullaun Stone
Where the kinsman of Nicholas Callan lies, professor
priest and electric pioneer.
Journey back to find the Norman Gernons, who came
nine centuries ago,
They built a church here, one of a kind.
Later other Lordships came and took their place.
Inevitable yield.
God bless all those whose bones lie in the shadow of
the windmill hill,
And the rhythmic fields of Cill in Cuile.

The birds murmur in peaceful territory, so green and
advanced.
We remember on the quiet sod.
Move in the memory fulfilled.

Bríd McDonnell

29

Columbine

Down the dripping lane to the hazel wood
I stop, startled as two pigeons burst
From a tree, exploding skywards.
My eye follows their smack and flap.

They plunge onto a green-grass clearing,
Step ungainly in a fantail flare,
Side step, waddle a dance apart,
Come close to coo and nibble.

On white-wing flash they fly to roost
In a shower-drenched cypress tree.
Puffball breasts thrust out, they
Nod and natter, peck and patter.

Down the dripping lane today
Blood marks a breast, a black eye stares.

Maureen Perkins

Commanders

You don't do the fighting; it's your boys,
Our sons, you send to die.
You haven't seen the blood, the pain,
Heard the gunfire, screaming men in the night.
A face of glory, strength, you raise
Your glasses to our boys, but what good
Is that to them, lying in state, wishing
Curses on the commanders who should
Be there at their side...

But I don't blame you for the wretched,
Twisted souls you have borne
The world; I don't blame you for the bullet
That killed that man, his sworn
Loyalty to you. You plan the fighting,
Strategy flows in your veins, a map to show
The way home. We trust you to keep us safe,
This wretched country. I know you know
What you're doing, just doing your job.

Kathryn Lambe

Country Woman On A Train

Ah the creature! See her sleep,
Her dreams filled of last week's deeds.
She's been to Dublin, and is all wore out.
Her shopping basket contains some wool,
Good intentions overcome by sleep.
Her overcoat of purple down,
Matching scarf as is her crown.

Her handbag is near at hand
To protect her from unruly men.
Trains as modern as can be.
May God bless CIE.
How does she stick this uncomfortable heat?
Her glasses still in place,
Despite the chattering of her teeth
Keeping time with the turning wheels,
As we move on into the night.

William Hayes

Crafted By Angels

Another year passes and you grow, ever beautiful
As those around you flutter endlessly, enchanted by
your spirit.
They live their days dancing before you, struggling for
attention
Even though they know not, the extent of your true
beauty.
The mind of the magnificence that is simply you, is
inconceivably breathtaking
With a heart that has never known the emotion of a
selfish beat.
You stand tall, elegant and refined, unique in this
predictable life
Graceful in opposing your unnecessarily confirmed
splendour.
A soul crafted by angels, purely modelled on their own
To captivate those blessed by seeing your true form,
your essence.
A moment in your presence rivals an eternity in the
heavens
But a lifetime in your heart, is where I hope to stay.

Raymond Boileau

Creation

I need for you to understand
When I say the things I do
And act the way I act, that
It is simply through frustration
Of not being able to love you true.
I don't mean to hurt you, upset or offend,
But instead want my soul to touch your heart
Want your heart to touch my soul,
And bring their warmth together as one.

If this is to be my final piece for you,
Lingering for eternity as the words that spoke forever,
I want you to know of your beauty, your absolute.
Your mind, body and soul, so complete
So effortless in their creation, in their life, your life.
That I am now, and will forever be, in awe of you.

My heart will continue to skip as you enter every room,
And my mind will race with the stars as they streak
                    across the sky
Waving their tails in salute of you from above,
Where one day you'll be safe in the heavens, from
                    whence you came.

You are truly an angel amongst the most ordinary of
                    souls,
Worth every precious moment, given you by time.

Raymond Boileau

Crete

Volcanic whispers echo around this isle,
as mountains and sea
exchange ancient dialogue;
Fragrant flowers perfume the air,
and a blistering sun
envelops the village.

One night, at Annapolis,
dancers performed,
This spectacle a microcosmic
mirror of Greece,
Crete's essence and purity
were distilled on stage,
as the audience reciprocated
with frenzied applause!

Jacqueline Bannon

Cró

They are not that blue, not angel blue.
Not sky-blue, they are ocean blue
- those eyes of yours.

It is beautiful, not typically.
Not overly-done, kind and warm
- that smile of yours.

It is that feeling, of course.
I feel it in my blood, forever more
- that heart of yours.

It is that deep, you know.
That special, to the end
- we will meet again.

Jessica Coyle

Crooked Man
(For 'B')

Isn't it you, befriender of the rejected
That for yourself rejects love?
Judged by self, found guilty,
On you love sits lightly, playful and kind
Afraid to filter through the dark soil of your soul.
Fearful of rejection at the deepest level.

Yet we, who know you, see what you cannot
The quality of the man is shining clear.
What is past is done and you are
Who you are today.
The cup, full to over-flowing is not beyond mercy
And what is evil does not attract nor give like you.

But there you are, heavy with the squandered painful
                              years.
Dear friend, dear friend, can't you see
God wrote the crooked lines of your life
In a firm and flowing hand!

Mary Kearns

Crumbling Misery

Wounded rock of thought
Knocked back and forth.
Crumbling hands of reason
Turning to dust.
Forgotten dreams and feelings,
Lost hopes and lost desires.
Can a man ever lose these or
Do they just die?
Shaking, shuddering, screaming
Lost in a place of no hope.
Alone, scared and myself,
Scrutinising every breath.
No bird of sin can help me
Destiny is without mercy.

Adrian Neasy

Dancing

Bodies swaying, music vibrating
Noise and smiling faces
What's this joy all around?
I can't tell
Pulsing, throbbing, all so strange
Hands waving, feet shuffling
Small spaces
More smiling faces
My heart races, hips gyrating
Bodies rotating
Hair is wet, must be sweat
Beat gets faster, I start prancing
Oh look!
We're all dancing!

Annette Donnelly

Dancing with Iomlanu

And once we were there, we trudged the world
In the countless millennia of conquest and struggling.
Our children were separated from the cosmos.
Still we are his only pride, her one joy, delight, their
only love.
It was when we had to be separated through our
differences the lovelight
Increased between us, waiting for the adversaries to
put away our swords.
The child would smile his smile of continued
Springtime.

Then there were those who, with their wings of
unconditional Summer
Never made May stay; as their arms stretched out to
the East, to the West
And let her fly...In their last, furious radiance of
abandoning love.
A spark of effervescent fire burned out in the skies.
Only pleasure remained.

Shh...I can see them in the woods now, the Normans.
I can hear their breath, with their women. Over here.
It's alright, it's alright, do you discern the farthest light
Through the distant trees? The pale faces, the
chainmail...
I never knew the cantering through the dark leaves....
Heaving the stunning joy...Of our birth, our baptism.
All infusing, never-ending, the sheer unutterable
beauty,
Of us all. Like our hearts beating,
Nothing, nothing can replace it, except our eternal
love.

Bríd McDonnell

Dawn At Proleek Dolmen

I follow the path that knelt its way
Down to the great stones, square shouldered
Stones standing for a thousand dawns.

No wind in the morning branches.
Sun rising over the Cooley hills,
Whitening gable ends of distance houses.

Sun reaching across the landscape,
Its rays, like fingers of some God
Pointing out the secrets the stones
Are hiding.

John Noonan

Day and Night

The simplest explanation for life is
that we are following the sun
from when it is born at dawn
to when it dies in the west at night.
A day in the life. Yes.
How long the night is
none can say, only
there is a moon and there are stars
so we must never be without some light.
The earth comforts its own.

Orla Fay

Death

A stranger in an alien land
I see their faces as I walk
They smile at me with empty eyes
They cannot know the way I talk.

I see them chatting in the street
I am no part of this
I long to be within their world
To be greeted by their kiss.

And yet I love my lonely place
To do just as I please
To keep the ice within my heart
Let no one hold the keys.

Death has come to those I've known
To leave me here at last
And this is what I sense they feel
They cannot know my past.

And so at last I walk alone
In places that I know
A stranger in an alien land
With neither friend nor foe.

Daphne Vernon

Distant Light

On a mild evening of soft
Falling rain
And falling light,

Branches of willow
Window frame a length of lake,
Lit smudged white.

A swan, casting a doubtful reflection, pressing
Forward quiet
Ripples, offering distant light.

As slow as he came he went,
His presence
A floating memory.

John Noonan

Doll-Faces

The sullen tears of a doll,
standing solemnly still,
still and straight and with
a look of sadness on her face.
Lines of pure-bred stitches
mapped and trapped and tapped
over beaded eyes of intense
adulation.
Pretence of smiles I see and taste,
white stained powdered faces
puffed, let loose on the shelf,
despaired and powerless.
They seize their makeshift
control, letting bells toll
on open courtyards rife with
chaotic opened strife, and
I see me.
Wishing I wasn't there at all.
My plan life foil unwrapped and
uncomfortable, taken aback with
dreams of wishing I was nothing.
Easy, simple and untorn.

Adrian Neasy

Dream

Here I lie alone, in darkness,
Silence surrounds me.
I'm lost in my own thoughts,
I feel myself drifting off into a dream....

I'm taken along the open fields,
Riding into the distance on horseback.
Not a care in the world,
I feel free.

For so long now I have felt tied down,
Crushed with all this hurt.
Never finding answers,
Is there hope, happiness, love?

But here as I lie alone in darkness,
I hear a whisper.....
"Ask those questions once again,
Right from the very start,
It's only you who knows the answers,
As they lie within your heart."

Peace robs my fear,
My dream is over...

Lydia Mullaney

Dressed To Kill

The bells rang out ominously,
announcing the midnight hour,
she excused herself
from her friends,
promising a hasty return.

From the corner of his eye he watched,
admiring her black clad back,
she turned to the stairway,
head thrust,
features set as she went.

Her long nails scarlet encased
in varnish like globules of blood,
her luscious lips slashed
with red lipstick,
betraying the thoughts in her head.

He edged towards the bedroom,
fear gnawing its way through his limbs,
clawing the wall
to elude her view,
seeking to escape, avoid his doom.

She delicately chose her footsteps,
teetering on black high-heeled shoes,
toes pointed like arrows
discharged from a bow,
heels dagger-like, narrow, reflecting her mood.

The moon moved through the room,
entering like a thief in the night,
casting strange shadows
through gloom,
as the curtains twitched in its light.

From his hiding place he watched her –

warily wending her way,
picking her baton
as she passed the bed,
muttering ceaselessly under her breath.

She pulled back the duvet,
looked under the bed,
checked behind doors,
for a clue where he'd went.
she knew he'd been here!
she'd sensed it as soon
as she'd spotted him earlier,
Leaving the bathroom!

But now was the moment –
the time he had dread!
as she threw back the curtain,
her murderous scream
could be heard –
and she battered the spider
until it was
DEAD.

Verna Keogh

Droichead Atha

Early morning hangs over
de Lacy's walled town.

A bell that rang
for work or prayer,
stays silent now
in Magdalene Tower.

The Tholsel clock chimes,
church bells ring out
in Georgian streets.
Gothic steeples soar.

Rumble of Cromwell's
cannonade echoes on Millmount,
drowns in the dark water
of the river Boyne.

Maureen Perkins

Drug Fit

The fear I felt inside that night on the beach,
We were looking at the stars, suddenly you fell at my
feet.
My heart raced, I thought you were dead.
Fear ran through your eyes,
Blood ran from your head.

You lay still, a heap on the ground
Eyes wide open, not making a sound.
I was scared, frightened, didn't know what to do,
Then you looked up at me,
I stared back at you.

"I don't know what happened...I'm okay now."
"Why did that happen? Please tell me how."
"I took something earlier; I only had a bit,
I really didn't think I'd end up like this."

And that was it over,
Nothing more was said,
We walked in silence,
Your hand held to your head.

After I saw you that night,
I began to realise,
Taking drugs does nothing
But abuse and ruin lives.

Your friends do it so you try it too,
You want someone to follow.
You'll go to bed, close your eyes,
You may never see tomorrow.

Lydia Mullaney

East of Eden

Autumn in the city of a thousand red lights
from afar a bed in the sapphire blue night
and I saw the ghost of James Dean pass my way,
smoke a cigarette just east of Eden.
And the moon could be rising
and we would be riding the stars
a million miles away,
far enough away to be alone,
to be solitary and blue like the night,
to be blue like freedom.
I could take your hand in mine
walking through the stars,
the million stars,
the million pretty stars
and they'd never be as pretty as your eyes,
your far away eyes,
your eyes of a galaxy,
a distant place.
All your whispers would be light,
beams to trip the heart
and we would fall like heroes
into the city,
into the city like a bed,
an earthly paradise,
fly immortal
before the sun came up
somewhere east of Eden.

Orla Fay

Easter King

Beauty is the shrine of awe
As God is seen there
His breath fills the blossom
with the fragrance of care

Now the hidden eye
Is wet with mercy's dew
The meltin' truth
makes man anew

And though he for souls
has peace to bring
How lowly comes
(The Easter King)

And what have we
as men to give
But strugglin' follow
as we live.

Pat Bennett

Ecstasy

This truly is fantastic!
A Queen I feel tonight.
I'm going to a place where enemies don't exist,
And time stands still,
And all this excitement from one little pill.
Another one or three, now everything is numb.
I'm feeling quite uneasy after biting on my gum.
Paranoia again - my fault!
Totally oblivious to the fact that -
I've let myself be taken away from all I hold dear,
A powerful force stripping away at my brain until
Eventually
I don't know whether to laugh or cry.
They're all looking at me - am I different?

- For this is a game of two halves
Where nobody wins and eventually
- We all COME DOWN.

Alison Maguire

Empty Chair

She stood,
There it was -
Regal in its majesty
Its tattered tassels trailing to the floor
Upright and righteous
Its back worn, torn and faded
Its arms still strong and sturdy
Ready to hold and mould
Her tears and fears
As it had in days of old.

She watched,
Touching and feeling
The flimsy fabric yielding
As her hands explored,
Willing it to feel
Soft and warm
Yet full of fun
Once more
As it had in days of old.

She sat,
The empty chair now full -
Fond flights
Of warm nights
By firelight
Her weary smile now lighting up her face
Remembering the days
When she was not alone -
Her gnarled grip loosening,
The loneliness lost
As she closes her eyes,
As she did in days of old.

Verna Keogh

Fairy Bush

It left no shadow
On the yellowed grass
Roots moved from darkness
To half moonlight
Leaning from sea to mountain
I dared not finger
Its rugged bark.
Three stout ditches
Spoke of bad luck.
The silent stars kept their distance.
Not quite centred
The leafless body
Gripped my breath
For a moment.
'You shouldn't be there',
My father voiced
From beyond the gate
'Best leave things be'.
Best leave untouched
That seeded by chance
Banished by the wise
To wisps and whispers.

Máire Larney

Famine Girl

Merciless she blows, straight from eastern shore
She robs us of our souls
Those screams, those cries
Never letting go, wakes us from our dreams
Timeless haunting melody
Always different, always new

Eyes as bright as diamonds
Slender a sight, cold as the night
Yet ceaseless tide it drowns our thoughts
Memories grow weak, years smother all trace
Only what is written on parchment in ink
Or spoken in language of dreams may we hear
'So long ago'

But yet she beckons my soul once more
Her ceaseless wail, her endless cry
How she stands, how she stares
How she rests by the sea
Carrying those sacks for all to see.

Her secret now safe in the grasp of the shore
To be blown, to be washed by the tides of the sea
Her soul now at rest somewhere close, never far
Forever happy, forever free
In dreams I still picture those bags by her shawl
That endless stare, feet are so bare
Cold as the wind from many a shore
We awaken once more.

Simon Scott

Farewell

Winge'd words waging war on weary ears
not ready to receive,
recoiling from tongues, feeding them
with fear.
Thoughts racing to and fro,
gathering momentum
In the frigid glow
of darkness turning to light.

To feel the ebb of life truly present
and yet –
creeping silently away,
Casting stealthy shadows in its wake.
Amid mortal moans
Of those not ready to accept,
waves wash weary
through the rocky shores,
as the winge'd bird ever skyward soars.

Verna Keogh

Favourite Things

I like touching many things
I love many soft things
Like the corner of my top
And the silk, soft, smooth of my top
I love touching many things
Slippery, slimy things
Like cleaning the slippery, slimy fish bowl
But I hate cleaning the stones from the fish bowl
I like the feel of many things
But best of all I love touching
Soft cats and dogs
I like the wet fur on their backs
I like licking the chocolate bowl
If I could have a day on my own
I'd spend it touching all my favourite things.

Tanya Thornton

Feet

Feet, you are important to me
And this is clear to see.
You guide me on my way through life
Sometimes on a road of struggle and strife.
You direct me to places of beauty and peace
Where all my troubled thoughts will cease.
At times you like to rest
Because you are tired
Or you're lazy and don't
Want to move or are afraid.
When this happens I ask the Lord for help.
He gives you renewed strength and courage.
Then once again you step out
With me to lead me to my
Destination.

Catherine Reilly

Flower Pots

My old wellie boots
Remember the days
We walked the fields,
I would rise up early,
Summon you, and off
We'd go at speed.

Autumn was special,
The old gnarled wood,
A kaleidoscope of colour
Through the veil of mist,
'Ere the sun had time
To burn it off,
And you reeking of
Cowshit and disinfectant.

Now I look at you,
Sentinels by the gate,
Resplendent in blooms,
With variegated ivy trailing
Till it touches your toes
And cheeky yellow pansies
For your crowning glory.

Maureen Kerrigan

Flux

I am everyone oh Cronos
even seamstress to a queen
stitched into every insect, twig and leaf
till two fish, locked in combat,
take us home.

Brendan Connolly

Flying Souls

I compare thee to a bird of prey
Flying the sky on a summer's day
Eyeing below for food to eat
People to see, people to meet

And when you turn your head above
You look to me like a soaring dove
White as snow, but hot as fire
Ice to calm a burning desire

And when at last you leave your trail
You remind me of a nightingale
Song so sweet, pain so deep
Eyes which cause mine to weep

And once you land at day's last spark
You look to me like a dying lark
Which leaves this world in tunes of woe
But I have hope that you'll not go

For in your heart you hold the key
To a soul which burns inside of me
And to unlock the burning light
You'll stay with me and end your flight.

Caroline McEvoy

62

For An Angel

(Dedicated to an angel,
Fiachra Humphreys 14/8/02 - 12/2/04)

Enveloped in a dense white fog
Like a curtain I can't part
I hear distant laughter, bright and easy.
I feel a vibrant presence
Fluttering, chasing, playfully swirling around me
I am filled with an incredible sense of elation
A serenity only heaven could ever know.
The curtain thins. Only mist now.
Soft as silken rain.
Sunlight sparkles through it.
I see colour. So bold. So rich.
It sears through thinning cloud and stuns my eyes.
Then I see you, my Angel.
So beautiful. So very beautiful.
Your radiance exploding sunlight in blinding flashes.
There is power here
Feel the tingle sparking on the air.
You are here. So innocent but so very strong
And as you fade through glimpses of light
You beam through the softest rain and my tears.
As you fly away, I hear the distant laughter
And your love shines down so brilliantly
Like spun sugar sparkling over the twists and curves of
silver.
You know how much you are loved,
How much you are missed.
Always on my mind.
Forever in my heart.
My Angel.

Lynn Dowling

For My Mother

I thought how it would be
if I saw you
walking along the street
with your black coat
and your green hat,
your head held high,
face smiling,
with its look
of shattered beauty.

How everything
would fall
into place again;
all the old familiarity
would return,
and all the unsaid things
could now be spoken.

But then I remembered,
the slow dissolution
the yearning to go,
and the grey hospital
on the grey March night.

And I knew
that never again
would you come
with the shopping bag
and the brown paper parcels
and the brown sticky toffees
for eager children's hands
and the quiet simplicity.

And I wondered
if in some green
        elysian field,
you were now
        dispensing
                your generosity.

Eileen Johnston

Forbidden Love

And if I could see you it would be love
Your eyes would shine like the stars above
Your lovely smile, your beauty rare
Our beating hearts without a care

As rains would fall, I'd clear your day
And take you past the Milky Way
I'd fly you through the heavens near
And show my love that I hold dear

Your smile of gold that makes me whole
My heart of love from which you stole
That curse of late will never leave
My temptress fair I cannot see.

Alison Magurie

Forgetting

Are there holes in my heart?
Black blood and black walls,
are my veins rotting
from forlorn falls?
A lonestruck lover of life,
caught out at sea
washing away tears of strife
with my own melancholy.
Driven mad with idle thoughts
Of love, life and shame.
Regretting spent time lost
On fake feelings of vain.

Shaken from despair of a monotonous love,
I spread forth my wings and fly like a dove.

Adrian Neasy

Forty Years

Forty years of marriage
Have come and they have gone -
But lately I have noticed
There's something very wrong.

A distance is between us -
I can't seem to explain,
The fire of love has burned right out -
Long silences remain.

We've landed in a comfort-zone,
And left marital bliss -
Is it no longer necessary
To greet me with a kiss?

What's the matter Paddy?
Don't you love me any more?
Is my body so far south
It's too repulsive to explore?

I went shopping in Ann Summers,
Doused my body with perfume -
But yet you stay as far away
As Taiwan is from Tuam.

I know I'm not the slim and sexy
Kathleen that you married,
But stretch marks are a given
When five children you have carried!

In the days when we were courting
You'd clasp me in your arms -
And young and foolish, I'd play up
To all your manly charms.

Remember how we met?
At that dance in Galway city:

You slipped your arm around my waist
Told me I was pretty.

I long for affection
For just a little fun.
But all I get is "Evenin' pet,
Is dinner nearly done?"

Angela Mullen

Fox

Sorry I disturbed you,
Gate-crashed your patch
You earned it hard
That half eaten snack

I know you're nearby
In yon thicket perhaps
Under the old stone wall
Rubbing shoulders
With blackthorn roots
Watching,
Waiting for me to move on

Only then will you return
Tentatively at first
Then bolder
To finish that tattered wing
And mangled ribcage.

Maureen Kerrigan

From The Sea
(For Millie and Lauren)

Born to the shore
Exposed to whatever
Seasons come,
Winter, Spring, Summer, Autumn
The sea shell, battered by Winter winds
Rain and snow, brittled by Spring's crisp air
Polished by the warm sunshine
Coloured by Autumn's glow.

Hoping no-one will come by and unsettle me
Like the child picking the best sea-shell
The lovers gazing into each other's eyes,
Walking anywhere
The old man or woman in deep thought
With memories of other times.
Times and the sea-shell hope to find
Its big black rock where it observes
The sky.
Land and sea, biding their time....
Sheltering bits fall,
Crack, chip,
Then slowly drift

Back to sea.

Tina McCormack Rafferty

Frost Made The Morning Perfect

Frost made the morning perfect,
Bone-white meadows welcoming our return,
Shaped by shock of hedgerow
And waters held at play,

The idle cast of broken tufts,
Risen like forgotten towns,
Haven of insect dreams
And seasons without regret.

Stories set down,
Deep among the smothering rush,
Cut warrens and setts
Sharding through ploughed plenty.

Brian Eardley

Genetic Engineering

Economic systems
Will decide
If you or I
Will live or die

A faulty gene
Will mean
Your sell-by date
Is near.

Spliced
Modified
Trimmed
To fit the corporate purse

Supervalue
Is the key
For a brand new
Super human being

Engineered
For all mankind
Virtue dies
While meekness lies

O Nature's seed,
You listless wimp
Can it be your force is spent
Or are you just too tired to think?

Bernadette Martin

God Is Life

God is life
Green shoots springing
From the dark rich soil
God is here
Within us all
Deep within our hidden soul
God is love
In wind and rain
He waits and listens for our call.

Forgive us God
Our wayward lives
Help us Lord to do your will.

Daphne Vernon

God's Recipe

God made the world, land and sea
Some animals that slither and snap
But He wanted some action, wanted some play,
So He made a grand little chap.

He took out a book, a really big book
Sequined with glittering ruby
But this isn't a book of the world and life,
It's a book of special recipe.

He took rats and snails and puppy dog tails
And some skin with a very light tan.
And with this He had now made
A nice bright smart little man.

God called this latest work of art
Adam now was he,
He put him to one side for now,
And started to make a she.

He took sugar and spice and everything nice
And a deeper shade of skin
And now He had just made
A beautiful little girl within.

He called this lovely woman Eve
And after this you see
He put them in the oven
At thirty seven degrees.

Sometime later God took them out
And what did He do next?
He put them on a conveyor belt
And put in the secret text.

From the belt beyond was a big machine
Which rumbled and grumbled aloud

Into which they would enter
And then they would be bound

With joy, bliss, fear and pain
Happiness I can tell
And next most importantly,
Abilities and talents as well.

And now you know how people are made
And how like Adam and Eve,
You have some talents of your own
That no-one else can thieve.

Like my talent is very simple
It is sitting here at home
Sitting at this very table,
Writing this very poem.

Dara Seoighe

Gypsy

Strange wanderlust fills
My gypsy heart
When winter sleet breaks away,
And though spring be led astray
Prophecy stills
My gypsy heart.

Old desires return
To stir the blood,
When bold winds begin to sing,
When geese migrate on blithe wing
Northward dreams burn
To stir my blood.

The distant hills call
Of enchantment,
My vagabond-road a plan
That follows the caravan,
Freedom my shawl

Of enchantment.

Adrian Saich

Halloween Creatures

Bushtail Bird

The bushtail bird may seem nice
With its beautiful feathers of leaves
But that bush on the very end
Will leave you in pain and grief

For that bush is crawling with
Thorns nettles and briars
And if you try to hurt it back
Please note they're very good fliers

Rhinocerosorus

The Rhinocerosorus looks like a rhino
But these are microscopic
But don't you now be fooled by them
Because they are diggaholic

They have a drill instead of a horn
And they live underground
So if you don't want a hole in your feet
When you walk don't make a sound

Fliddlyflinks

Fliddlyflinks are like pixies with wings
Only these are made of wood
And if you want one as a pet
Well this is what you should.....

Take the one whose wood is oak
Because that's what my name means
And if you put them on the wall
Afraid of heights they'll scream

Slumpsia

The slumpsia is a small gooey mould
That slips and slops around
But don't think size is everything
Because it can go underground

It can slip into the ceiling and into the walls too
So if you don't watch your step
It could slip right into you

Darrira

The darrira is like a little horse
But it has ears like a rabbit
And if it is really happy
It does this strange little habit

It starts to change its colour
Orange green and white
All the colours in the world
Some dark and some bright

Dara Seoighe

Hands

Hands, you are very precious to me.
There is great power in you,
In everything you do.
Your touch is gentle and loving.
You reach out to people;
You inspire me to develop
The Lord's talents, God's gifts given to me.
You hold the gifts I bring to others.
I write with you.
I work with you.

Catherine Reilly

Hell-Shaped Reality

Plundered soul
robbed and raped of life,
Policeman's bell tolls
rescuing me from slumber.
Nightmare clashing reality
Hell gripped shackles
on my feet.
Facing hells fury,
life hath no meaning,
thy lasting scream until death
following until that last breath
is gone.

Skull ridden paradise,
trampled by the herded thoughts,
cramped squatters of sin
skewing out vomitous reason.
Reason of sin?
Reason of life?
Reason of being?
The freedom of life
is to be found
with goodness and feelings
of love marching forth bound
with radiant sunshine of
velvetous squealing
of thy inner child.

Adrian Neasy

His Farewell On Holy Brigid's Hill *

Thus far the hound has endured,
Hound of Culainn, Hound of Ulster,
a long and costly and furious road!
This handful of years,
nineteen or twenty!
'A beardless youth!'
they called me, fearful but envious!
Many of those are lost in darkness,
others survived to yap like curs
at the heels of this intrepid hound,
weakened perhaps by loss of blood,
and wounded and alone! Yet I hope
and swear, whenever The Reaper comes,
alone I'll mount the Grey-of-Macha
and drag them into the Dark Valley!
that none may celebrate my defeat
with flourishes of drinking horns! Rather,
let them recall, 'The hound was best
of all the heroes of Craobhrua!
The Hound was brightest of Scathach's pupils!
He killed whoever blocked his path!
He spared nothing, and no-one, for Ulster!
The Hound, sling-in-hand, held
The Gap o' The North against the invader!
The Hound, for Ulster, killed his friend!
and never feared the Mor-Riogan!'
Finally, I stand at this stone,
my last of too few friends!
May all who hear, remember this:
'The Hound spared nothing for Ulster!'
farewell on Holy Brigid's Hill!!

*Remembering his death at Knockbridge, outside
Dundalk.*

Tom Hamill

81

Homage to Delilah

She stretches her limbs
heavenward,
Exuding pale cherry-blossom
like old Hollywood charm;
A sentinel in this Spring
orchard.

Season by season, her
chameleon tendencies enrapture
my vision,
She's a sacred symbol;
A liminal portent of the
otherworld.

From skeletal winter branches,
She metamorphoses to visions
of grandeur.
Blackbirds and thrushes
caress her leaves,
And she listens eagerly to
their song.

Jacqueline Bannon

Horse

I want a stable to stay in
when it's raining
when it's cold
and especially when it's snowing.

I hate staying out in this field.
I get all wet and mucky
and it annoys me
getting washed.

I hate my owner
for leaving me here
in this field
when it's really cold.
Look around!
All my friends are inside
nice and warm.
I wish I were like them.

If only my owner could see
that I'm cold and lonely
on my own.

Doreen Browne

House of Integrity

The house is
Called
INTEGRITY
To Integrity
Come
Young men women
Free-willed but anxious
Off the street
Fleeing
Own desire for
Speed, pot junk.

The bright-faced
Youngsters who
Welcome us to
Their open house
Show us
Proudly how
They have
Redeemed discards
Resurrected
Dingy rooms with
Bright paint
Earnest sweat
Determination.

We
Admire ingenuity
Neatness and order
Listen
To a rock combo
Home-made cake
My Mind
Goes back
To an alley by a movie theatre
I used to pass on my
Way to work early morning

Four Junkies
Three men and a woman
Met there to wait
To wait shivering
For a Fix
They were gaunt
Unbelievably gaunt
Sucked dry
Like the pale
Skins of cockroaches in a
Neglected cupboard.

The quietly pleasant
Young man who
Has been showing us
Around
INTEGRITY
Presses my hand
Saying
Goodbye
Thank you for coming.

My eyes are
Suddenly
Tight and hot
With tears
For that instant
My hope for him
Burns
Burns as fiercely as
Ever
His own must have.

Adrian Saich

I Tell You These Hills

I tell you these hills know how to keep a secret.
Carved in song and men's prayers
And washed through with memory...
The sour bread of history
Taking earth as an easel
Sullen of soul, riven with chance waters,
Deep in drumlin lore
Coal-black and hungrier than night...
Fields forged in the slenderness
Of crumbling seasons
The sickle blade cutting through time

They are wells without sorrow...
The springs that feed today....

Brian Eardley

I Was Dead Once...Gently Stirred

They stood there, bleak and cold,
as if around a campfire that had lost its flame.
They complained earlier about the absence of my old,
strapping themselves with blame.

The coffin long and narrow,
not enough room for me to breathe,
soft and satiny, cold as marrow,
time passed at a tortoise's speed.
The wind howling, rain beating down,
ground sodden, sad as hell.
My family, my friends, the troubled crowns
Pray and pray with some blessed spell.
I am dead, black,
black as the ground they put me in,
evil demons, earthworms and maggots crawling,
tap-tapping on my wooden house.
The grating of wood against the rocks,
The never-ending sound of tick-tocking clocks,
Ticking on now, not one breath shall ever be mine.

She called me, I began to stir,
resurrected from my lonesome grave...
one change it seems was all it took,
to wake me from her dreadful place,
living now, just like the lone sky,
awaken, awaken...

Adrian Neasy

I'm No Genius

I'm no genius.
I never come first.
I never win prizes or cups.
I can sing and dance a bit.
But not good enough to win prizes or cups.
I can do the washing and iron the clothes.
But whoever heard of prizes for that.
I can dig the garden, shovel the clay.
Dig holes and spray.
But they don't give prizes for that.
I can knit and sew, make jumpers and suits, cushions
                         and covers.
In all the latest designs.
But they never give cups or prizes for that.
I can wash the dishes, the pots and pans.
Make them sparkle and shine.
But no thanks or prizes for that.
I can do the cooking.
Bake bread, gateaux and cakes of the highest quality.
Which never last long enough to win prizes or cups.
I can paint the ceiling, walls and doors, clean the
                         windows
And polish the floor.
But they don't give cups or prizes for that.
I can do the shopping and carry the bags.
Mind the children and feed the dog.
But whoever heard of prizes for that.
One thing I know.
I will never be redundant or receive redundancy pay.
But who knows.
I might get a first prize in the slave section.
Without reward, cup, or bouquet.

Sheila Lynch

I'm Sorry That I Killed Your Cat

Dear Ms Marples,

I'm sorry that I killed your cat
There in your driveway where it sat.

I didn't mean for his poor head
To end up in the flowerbed!

If only I had seen the creature,
His two eyeballs would not now feature

All over your garden path,
Like some horrific aftermath.

His ribs, I think I dislocated.
His poor tail, it was more ill-fated -

It got entangled in my tyres,
(I've since removed it with a pliers)

But I'm sure he was already gone
Before his legs were dragged along;

He had taken his final breath
Before I squished him to his death.

I tried to gather up his corpse
(A complicated task of course!)

I tied the pieces back in place.
(Sorry I couldn't fix his face)

I'm sure, the feline you will miss.
I do apologise for this.

What can I say to ease your pain?
You'll never hear his purr again.

But as you place him in his grave,
Just think of all the milk you'll save!

Don't cry Ms Marples! Don't be sad!
His final moments weren't that bad.

I reassure you, as a friend,
Your Trixy had a peaceful end.

Sincerely -
Your neighbour,
Mr Peter Jones.

Angela Mullen

Identity Crisis
(For Rev. Eamon Treanor)

A philosopher monkey
Sat in a tree
Masters in psycho and
Pea haith dee
Choosing to ponder
From panther to bee
Why many confuse their
Identity.

First appointment today,
In sheer desperation,
One animal sought this
Renowned meditation
What's wrong with me Doc?
I'm going mad with frustration
You don't think I might need
A small operation?

To do all the things
I need to, each day
The difficulty is,
I can't get away
The birds keep me busy
From dawn to sunset
By then I'm too tired and
Feeling upset
They squawk and they clamour,
Their demands never end
Their needs are so mighty,
I'm hard to defend.

Tell me my friend,
Why be stuck in this groove?
You're a very fine fellow,
I don't disapprove,
I have often observed you,
And have to confess

I question the reason
YOU'RE building a nest...

I'm willing to help,
But there's never an end
When there's a problem,
It's for me that they send.
I'm stressed out, resentful,
I'm not up to the job
Sorry if I seem a bit of a slob.

But inside I'm different
So calm and so strong,
And there's no one with whom
I don't get along.
Still I can't help but feel,
Maybe it's selfish to say
That with me all the animals
Have their own way.

You're wrong if you think
Like the birds, that you're small
With no-one to measure,
You can't see how tall!
Feel your strength, raise your voice
They will all fly away
When you stretch out your limbs
At the start of the day.

Thanks for listening Doc Monkey
How much do I owe you?
Just wrap your trunk round
This tree and I'll show you!

For a big bird,
I'm just doing my job in the end.....

YOU'RE NOT A BIRD, YOU'RE AN ELEPHANT,
MY ESTEEMED FRIEND!

Mary Kearns

If I Were A Star

If I were a star, high up in the sky,
I wouldn't shine over this bleak countryside.
I'd range across Europe at the speed of light,
All over the world in only one night.

I'd shine for the Pharaohs in the Egypt of old,
I'd remember by heart each story once told,
I'd shine in wet forests; I'd shine on white sands,
I'd shine through great cities, through bleak famine
lands.

I'd light a dark ocean for the ghost ships of time,
I'd shimmer a story, a song and a rhyme,
I'd twinkle a glimmer of hope in dark skies,
Watch the course of each planet through glittering
eyes.

So while other stars zoom through the magical ages,
Through deserts of time where the wild wind still
rages,
I thank all the stars, way up in the sky,
Who choose to shine over my own countryside.

Rachel Brennan

If You Should Enter

If I should dream beside the glowing embers
When the entire world is far removed from me
I could forget those bitter bleak Decembers
If I should hear you enter quietly
Then if you paused one moment by my armchair
You need not speak a word but I should know

Consider long my love before you enter
For I am sure I'd never let you go.

Adrian Saich

If You Will Just Be One With Me

Everywhere in everything
My being
In seed and seas, birds and bees
I am

In word and deed
I'll dialogue with thee
If you will just
Acknowledge me

Legged, winged
All living things
Your tears are just
A path to me

Access is where
I'll need to be
If you will just
Be one with me.

Bernadette Martin

In Another Time

In another time
Where rainbows water colour play
I reach out my hand to you in silence.

In another time
Where waves dance on moon drenched sands
And stars blaze out free
I make silver linings with your clouds.

In another time
I sit with you in the magic hush of early morn
To watch the sun on rosy golden wings illuminate the
ocean.

In another time
I walk with you through confetti showers of crocus
To give your soul delicate wings to soar to affectionate
airs.

In another time
Where night whispers softly
And the moon smiles down at you sleeping
I will spin your dreams and enchant you
For you have touched my heart for always.

Lynn Dowling

96

In The Beating of a Heart

About a month ago in a graveyard close by
Where silence lives alone
Stood two souls, once lost, now found.
A warm, sun drenched breeze
Wrapped my face in its delight
Without warning, opening my eyes.
I found myself staring, shaking, wondering
Side by side the woman I love
Realising how good it felt, we felt, she felt.
A feeling, an urge, suppressed
Long before for fear of repercussion
Returned, bringing with it, the joys of hope.
I could see her by my side
Struggling to stare directly ahead
Knowing of the looks I gave to her.
She seemed to be creating thoughts
Just for thoughts sake
Just to drown out her forceful desires.
Maybe it was the serene beauty of the moment
Coupled with her majestic air
Knowing it was just the two of us and the world.
But as the winds blustered for our attention
Giving sound to each and every silent thought
And life to imaginations running, together, wild.
We knew of each others feelings
In this quiet graveyard, on that day of days
Silenced by our silence, I wanted nothing more than to
kiss her.

Raymond Boileau

Innocence

Just imagine
If Eve
Had not taken a little bite
Just imagine
Perfect bodies and peace
And on your brow
Not a drop of sweat
Just imagine

Peter Louet-Feisser

Invisibelle

Sum up the energy –
it beats
fire red and lightening blue.
I hold it in my hand.

Sparks that crackle and twist,
like electricity
jump from me.

The power, the height, the volume of my voice.
The heat radiating from my heart,
hot enough to burn those who do me wrong,
and make them listen to what I have to say.
The acceleration and encompassing noise
reeling from this orb of light –
Fly up, fly down,
may it shoot you in the spine,
Turn around and now finally look and see,
I have strength now, may it grow infinitely.

Yvonne Kelly

Island of Dreams

My island of dreams I cherish dear,
But for its future I have a fear,
That a blue-eyed baby just like me,
Grows up perfect but has to see,
The religious divide that exists in each heart,
One side or another we all play our part,
Drumcree's little cottage with its orange sunset,
Where a boy and a girl from both sides once met,
Westport House as it stands, waves crashing nearby,
The violence and hurt, we ask ourselves why.

The summer nights come, the bonfires burn,
I think and I pray that the tables will turn,
So the sun it can rise and spread its fine rays,
To the beauty and truth in the rest of our days.

Eugenia Thompson

Jet Plane

Turbulence, the journey begins,
Some miles ahead, proceeding
The billowing smoke and wings;
The space vast.

The sound, generates another,
Illusion of the destination
In full flight and later;
Runway meets wheels.

Landing swift, and then arrival
Tolerate the baggage for
Journey home, unpack from
The jetplane of Life.

Jessica Coyle

Journey

God bear me the strength,
To walk this rocky road.
The thorns excruciate the journey,
The hardening weight of my weary load;
Those heavy storms have burdened,
With a dampened heart that's been denied,
This child was almost forgotten,
And left alone without a home,
And crying by the wayside.

Oh grant me peace, I humbly pray,
I call upon thee now,
And hear my voice, my pain, my name,
Please recognise my vow.
For which you gave me yesterday,
Or days belonging before,
You gave me life, my destiny,
You planned I'd find this door.

Oh yearning to remember,
The spiritual strength I feel,
And calling to surrender,
For the wounds are yet to heal.
For when the night extenuates,
And morn seems oh so long,
Away with all the memories,
Still vivid, still so strong.

Oh will I martyr to this cause,
Or shall I stand and fight?
And would you grant me liberty,
And pardon for my rights.
You know me true, like none before,
And too, I at ease with thee,
But will it be forever more?
And for all eternity?

For tired eyes are weepy
From crying in the rain,
A convincing guise from all who spy,
And gossip for my shame,
The child has grown anonymously
With an aged and sullen face,
But has known such lonely agony,
An outcast, exiled with no place.

And true to form as years ago,
Beyond days of bitter sweet,
Those memoirs haunt from which they know,
And linger till we meet.
For I have known the wings of love,
The saviour from loss and pain,
To fly aboard and hover above,
My soul is destined to acclaim.

Somewhere buried deep inside
And hidden in the psyche,
There is a map; my life's design,
For this path on which I journey.
So continue on this road shall I,
Directed by the winds,
My soul has called; my name was spoken,
The curse I carried has finally broken.

Clare Ana Lalor-Fitzpatrick

June Morn

Waiting to hold
This essence of morning...

Witness to the winged prayer
Of summer insect song,
The wild Bragan backbone
Portsteeped in nightdark bog water
Dusty pines in slow sway
Upon the mountain song

Heady on the blunt musk
Of pasture and brook,
Eager for the August uprush
Sudden and unconquerable,
Melded hedgerow play
Kiss of colour and light,

Our jade kingdom....
Our secret dream....

Brian Eardley

Lady Lavery

How poorly you look
You that only a month ago
Looked so proud and stately
But your travels took you
To very strange places
And have taken their toll

You were never the same
Since that wet fair day, when
You fell in cowshit whilst
The dealer and the farmer
Haggled over the price
Of a suck calf

The dealer picked you up
Spat on you, and wiped your face
In the arse of this trousers.
Next day his wife took you
To the supermarket
Where no one complained
About your colour or B.O.

Maureen Kerrigan

Lady's Handbag

Hacked from pillar to post
My work is never done
My owner's just a simple lass
I'm now a bulging mass

Stuffed from head to toe
And ugly to behold
Stripped of any kind of dignity
My insides sticking out

A gaping open mouth
Disgorge implements
Lethal sharp and blunt
Household bills, tampons
Indignity complete

Worn out from wear
My cracked and leathery skin
Once a shiny black
Is now a faded grey

A broken strap
My once proud shoulders
Lopsided, unseemly
I was not meant for such a life

And when my day is done
I'm kicked right out of sight
Unsavoury bedfellows
Sensitivity recoils

Bottom up, I now lie
On top of a rubbish heap
Decomposing companions
I vie for space unshamed.

Bernadette Martin

Lake-Side Reed

(For Christabel)

The whispering reeds are many,
A million blades of every green;
We see them all, but never any
As an individual, long and lean.
I studied one, a single stem,
And counted fourteen different shades:
A simple natural emerald gem,
Beneath the feathery willow-glades.
It's reflection, in sunlit waters,
Completely mirrors to its stalk;
The haunt of herons, coots and otters,
And the silent quartering hawk.
I bent to pluck the helpless reed,
To press it in a book;
But realised the innocent deed,
Would spoil what I had took.
So, I left my new-found friend,
And wandered on my way.
A lovely reed, a living gem,
To fringe that lake-side bay.

Nicholas Kearns

Layers

Time fogs but for all that we are
We can never be free from its clutches
Levels collect, then surely turn to dust
Just as iron turns to rust
Collective they bind, by the soul are combined
Released from the hour glass, forever set free

Traces remain of life long retired
Thousands of thousands remain
Long set free for our dreams to pursue
Add to collections with glee
Channelled through levels in stone they are trapped
A new dimension in vision released

Text of ruin, of homework destroyed
To repair, to combine, shall we enter this frame
Some will dive at the chance
Others try in vain
Many remain in wait for decay
Most of us pray for forgiveness today.

Simon Scott

Leprechaun's Fire

Let's burn a hole in the dark
And make the rainbow an arc
Above a leprechaun's fire
We must see where we go
For heave and for hoe
Before the song of the Briar

We have pots we have pans
In which nothing is man's
With dew that comes from the Briar
And seven of Eireann's fine cooks
With the ancient of Books
For the feast of a leprechaun's fire

To you Gauneen* I've clung
Since the first bell was rung
From the forge of McGuire
Who sent poppin' in
A goose with no chin
To lay at a leprechaun's fire

Now Gauneen my dear
Clopper is here
Horse of the gallopin' friar
He knows he can sup
To a turkeys hiccup
Before he returns to the mire

We have hay we have straw
Till the arctic shall thaw
With a notion of volcanic desire
A hoof-run nut enough
Till steamin' with guff
To tale of the hunter's fire

I Gauneen with that half moon fish
Seven onions from a Bogmans fire

Are taken down with an emerald crown
To the swan in the lily-duck choir

Bring the harp of wild mirth
Lets shoe dance the earth
In the glow of the coals desire
Hush ye swine from the herd
Who are deeply disturbed
Dryin' pig tails at the fire

An oul' who-bird and raven
Came with two goats unshaven
And a peacock the eye could admire
Seven ghosts were allowed
To dance in the crowd
Banshees are kept from the fire

On the broad pans of jisell
Snakes curl to a sizzle
Charmers have fled from the fire
Seven died of a chough
Before they took off
Callin' a leprechaun liar

Tho' we're a merry wee bunch
With poteen and munch
Tho' best from the clans desire
Were we to behave
Like those for the grave
It would cost the whole empire

Now dawn's come about
And the rabbits are out
And the birds sing to Thorney O'Briar
The grass is as green
Not a cinder is seen
Flowers are the blaze of a leprechaun's fire.

*leprechaun wife

Pat Bennett

Listening Now

Listening now...
I can hear his voice,
The airy lilt
Steeped in sorrow,
Ready for song
Or story...

Looking now...
I can see his face,
The soulmarks and etchings
Of life set in flame,
Ready, always ready
For more...

Brian Eardley

Little Flower

Long from the womb of summers that were happy,
long the days.
Wait for me wait, my sister. I cannot reach the elves'
heaven
While materialistic. Envious once I call out
continuously
From a covertly secret place, call out to you, my once
little friend.
Day and night, night and day the blind struggle of
work continues,
Would you were here, Therese, little darling.

You visited each of us, with a tenacious affection.
Your charm and wit and innocence touched us.
And we miss you, miss you so much with our
splintered souls.
No amount of crying can bring us back to where you
once were.

Once in a troubled springtime you held my hand.

Wouldn't deny you heaven with Jesus by your side.
Wouldn't deny you the fantastic unity of all our souls.
And wouldn't deny you your omnipresence and
understanding now.
We loved you once, we cry out, you love us back
eternally.

Love was all you ever believed in while on earth. So it
will be.

Bríd McDonnell

Lost In Grafton Street, At Four

Daddy in one hand, ice-cream in the other:
Life is perfect.

I rescue sweet melting vanilla drops
As they hang for dear life
From a wafer cliff.
The April sun laughs and tickles my cheeks.

The street performer lures me in -
His juggling act now in full swing,
Coloured balls, spin before me -
Red, Yellow, Green -
And are caught by swift hands.
He moves on to fire.
Orange flames, scorching heat,
Are no match for his magic -
They dance to his beat.
He catches my gaze and throws me a wink,
Just like Dad does.

Dad!
Did his hand forget mine
In his rush to the bank?
Sudden panic shoots through me, adrift in a sea
Of unfriendly legs and bright shopping bags -
Abandoned.

Standing at Bewley's, I seek out khaki shorts
And grey socks with sandals.
But I find Daddys everywhere! None of them mine.

My ice-cream cone crashes head first
To its grave, bleeding raspberry ripple
On the red bricked pave.
Tears leave my eyes as I cry
For both losses.
How will life be now

I'm an orphaned child?

Suddenly airborne, my feet leave the ground
In my father's arms I'm spinning around!
Like the juggling balls.

'There you are girl! Don't tell this to your mother.
You dropped your ice-cream? Well let's get you
another!'

Daddy in one hand, ice-cream in the other:
Life is perfect.

Angela Mullen

Lough Ramour

Below is the end of the lake
Studded with islands, and each island
Is like a mound of greenery
So thickly do the trees grow together.

In the autumn when the different
Hues come on the foliage,
Each island looks like
A big pompom set in the water.

The surface of the lake
Is smooth enough to reflect
The blue sky, the fleecy clouds,
The leafy glory of the trees and ferns.
All these hues mingle in the depths
Gilded by the glad sunshine
That fondly embraces all.

Maureen Kerrigan

Loveliest of Poets

Loveliest of Poets, your words are to me
Like the beautiful blossom upon the cherry tree,
Each syllable you choose with the music of your words
Flows from my lips like the singing birds.

To honour your wordsmith, I planted a tree
In the garden of my house for man, woman,
                    children to see,
I thought the five vowels a perfect name plaque
So I carved the first two and I left it like that.

As spring does come, but once a year
Counting a life in springs is too short I fear,
When winter comes and the cherry's flower is gone
I read your poem and the cherry blossoms on.

Cyril Nolan

Madrid

The wind sings a
Desolate song
For those who did
Not survive
The storm that came
Violent, sweeping strong
When evil
Spreads its wings
Like a bird
Of prey
Suddenly, in the morning
Making black the day.
Now, the world weeps
With Spain

Laura Bruce

Many Septembers

I have fallen slowly to my knees, like the leaves
to the ground this September evening,
many times. Many Septembers
have heard winter's whispering.
I have seen the dappled yellow through the green
                                    leaves
fattening branches that will become bare as a bone.
I know that a long winter walks to us out of time
wearing shades of cool wind and rain
though there is yet blossoming fruit,
blackberries, apples and unyielding crop.
There will be a careful surrender to the season,
a golden reign of wheat will be trembling topple
into it's earthly hill side bed of summer sleep
where roots, to flower, drank soil deep.
Again now it is a prayer for strength and peace of mind
amid the autumnal fragmentation of a poem.
And the knowledge that there is something greater and
                                    divine
than a single life causes my brief genuflection.
Maybe it is life itself.

Orla Fay

Master's Class

He sits
at the wheel
prayerful
as a Zen monk.

Through masterful hands
landslides of clay
slip and slide
form slowly.

In a spin
of mind, heart and soul
to combine
in a perfect design.

Awed
students watch
all hoping to find
the artist in themselves.

But knowing enough
to feel the lifeblood
in the clay.

Thomas Clarke

Meadowsweet

Yes, I am part of God
God is multi-cultural
I am an orchestra

He is one with many names
With many faces
He is one
I am one
With many names
With many faces
I am one

I am a one day flower
I see it for the first time
I see it for the last time
I am a one day flower
In all my glory
Tomorrow I am gone
No less glorious

Peter Louet-Feisser

Mellifont Abbey

The Abbot goes early as dawn allows,
Back over thistle fields where cows
Rise and stretch as he passes.

Arriving now, after Monks have vanished
From the ruin,
The Abbot finds an altar of ragworth,
(This morning in a haze of midgets)
Bows his head, pours out Latin prayers
That echo back over the stone vestry.

Pigeons and blackbirds fly out of ivy, leaving
Coldness between ancient prayer and ruin,
Except for morning's opening, into eastern sun.

John Noonan

Memories Old Memories New

Memories old, memories new
Gather round the heart
Pull you through and fro
Some too painful to connect with alone
Some too beautiful make you want to
      shout

Dreams old you should have made reality
Dreams new give hope to start afresh
Prayer of old muttering under breath
Not connecting
Prayer of new singing from soul
Or cries of pain from the heart

Wishes of old never came into frame
Wishes of new upon rainbows of age past
Connected to wings of hope
Lift the spirit of old
Breathe new life upon
Withered frail soul

New spirit soars above all storms of life
Takes flight to cloudless new horizons
Gathering comfort at last
New spirit is free
Thanking God so good to send one who
I know will not take offence
Feel disgust
As my heart opens
Revealing all

Jenny Hagan

Monopoly

There are no rules,
no walls or guides,
to what we each
must feel inside.

No rods dictate
the words we speak,
no thoughts provoke
how weak is grief.

The feelings felt
when hearts are broke -
Externally,
how well we cope!

Through smiles at day
to tears at night,
thoughts not paraded,
steered out of sight.

From dark recesses
at eventide,
our thoughts are pulled
from deep inside.

Through wildest storms
and childhood thief,
there is no monopoly
on grief.

Verna Keogh

Moon Sleep

Over midnight fields, white moon pulling
Clouds blanket from its face that rests
On the dark pillow of the night sky.

Walking my way home over the river
Running silver, catching tonight
The moons glow, stretching out its round
Round distant light.

Clearing again above treetops, brighten into
A vastness, whitening fields and hollow,
A roadway, our house, the room where you
Lie sleeping, curtains leaking milky light,
It attends your face sleeping on the pillow,
Reviled by a scattered cloud of
Dark hair.

John Noonan

Morning

The sunlight on the water
The molton gold of day
Dawn in all its glory
Like life, not here to stay.

The beauty God created
He gave to us to hold.
So often now unnoticed,
Destroyed when truth is sold.

Golden, golden sun
Heavenly, heavenly morn.
Pathway across the water
Awakening to new dawn.

Daphne Vernon

My Angel

Today in a quiet country graveyard
Where sun drenched grasses gently sway
I spoke with an angel.
In a tranquil peaceful haven
Where light breezes whisper like a silent prayer
He stood before me.
With the clearest, most beautiful eyes and sun kissed
hair
He took my hand and gently smiled
A smile that illuminated the heavens.
Through a million tears I hold his gaze
Searching, seeking, questioning.
I focus on his rosebud lips
As he softly speaks to me.
I feel his wings around me now, so soft, comforting
Holding me close to him, so tight, so near.
My soul warms.
Time stands still. Just for us.
In these precious moments
In the silence of the graveyard
An angel touched my heart.

Lynn Dowling

My Father's Grave

Some people ask me why I do not visit,
The grave wherein my dad is laid to rest.
I'd rather wander with his spirit
Through all the hills that we loved best.

We knew the secrets of the woodlands,
And how each feathered friend would build a nest.
We lived the rule of flowers for the living,
And understood that rule would stand the test.

But now that he is gone and left me
I keep his memory locked within my heart.
I share his thoughts through kindred spirit,
And do the things I know that he'd like best.

So when you see some lonesome stranger
Who doesn't visit tombs for show,
Don't criticise his errant ramblings,
His heart is filled with longing pain, I know.

Adrian Saich

My Feelings

I feel happy today
Bright white and shiny
Inside I feel like a puppy
Jumping up and down
And wagging its tail
I wish it could last forever!

Niall McDonagh

My Grave

I'd like a tree to mark my grave
An evergreen so tall and fair
A shady canopy in summer
And shelter from the harsh winter

Where the blackbird could come and sing
From his lofty perch announcing spring
The song thrush could build her nest
And rear her brood without fear or threat

Little squirrel might curl up
And sleep without bit, bight or sup
All through the harsh cold winter
In the bosom of sweet lumber

Big strong roots to enfold me
And guide my spirit to paradise.

Maureen Kerrigan

My Nanny

My nanny's turning eighty; it's a milestone in her life,
Always a terrific mother, and a loving wife,
This is a happy time for us as we celebrate the day,
To show how much we love her, in a special kind of
way.

Nanny loves her garden, it's plain for all to see
With lavender, roses and lots of rosemary.
In her eighty years she's travelled to places far and
near,
Enjoyed her life, laughed a lot, but also shed a tear.

She gave everyone of us so much happiness and joy,
Giving birth to seven girls, and also to a boy.
They say that wine improves with age and I'm sure
you'll all agree.
Tonight the same is easily said of our eighty year old
Nanny.

Niamh Fanning

My Ocean

Open your mind and let me die,
Still I can feel your evil eyes,
Evil eyes that I despise.

Trapped in your gaze of denunciation,
Void of clue and void of notion
Trapped in a wordless imagination.

Stranded in the deepest ocean.
A melting pot of pure emotion.

Fearing I won't see tomorrow as
I'm drowning deep in sorrow.
Grabbing out if just to borrow
The sanity I was blind to see.

But I can't reach it for eternity
As it's too far for my eyes to see.
Thus now treading always dreading
The vast expanse in front of me

Begging and pleading to be set free.
I know of course in heart of hearts
Begging won't help me.

For the ocean in which I am trapped
Is also trapped in me.

Thomas Hynes

My Old Friend The Snow

My eyes shone with delight,
As a smile spread across my face,
The surprise of seeing snow
On Christmas morning last,
Like a new birth
Awoke my inner child.

A shroud of snow transformed my world,
Into a pure and innocent place
This new lightness transported me,
Happy memories sprinkled back
Suddenly I was a boy again
Playing in the snow.

I put on my woollen hat and gloves
To shake my old friend's hand
Stopping at the doorway
My inner child, tugged
As not to disturb the snow
Stepping carefully along the path,
I still stare in wonder at my footprints.

There's something simple, something childish,
In seeing the sole's imprint upon the snow,
Like a divine touch, when the snow thaws
The imprint will remain,
My warm memories will melt the coldest days
When I see my old friend the snow again.

Cyril Nolan

My Son

(I Know Where You Are!)

When I heard about you in the race
I couldn't look you in the face.
When I said you were a disgrace
You got up and packed your case.

I waited and waited to hear from you
But you slept outside
And never came home to show your face.
But your report from school was great!

I remember when you said your first word,
Learned to tie your shoelace
Your first day at school
And you won your first race.

But the day the phone rang
And I heard the bad news,
I put on my coat and
Ran over to you.

The car was all bent and
The windows all cracked;
It was then I saw
Your face was all smashed.

So many lives lost
Not only these known
But many lives lost
So close to home.

Stephanie Fennell

Mythology of a Field

The muddy field envelops a shining pool;
Enchanted water reflects iridescent colour,
Mists shroud sheep-shades in the fields,
And the forest assumes a self-imposed authority.

Do I witness Artemis admire a deer?
Myriad trees withhold centenaries of secrets,
Dunsany Woods beckon from my window,
But first, I must observe my reflection in the shining
water.

Jacqueline Bannon

Nature Dance

Tonight a brilliant moon appeared
And slowly hid away
The stars that waltz in ballroom sky
Along the Milky Way
But brought instead an awesome view
Of treetop silhouettes
And pines linking arms with firs
In graceful minuets.

Our God has made this universe
A beautiful parade
Of lovely moving nature things
That dance his serenade.

Adrian Saich

Neolithic

Memories of yesterday ascended on his forehead now,
Making him weary. The eastern gales from Irish Sea
Came close, whirling outside the tomb where Naide lay
        low
With the other deceased. A low-pitched voice opened
        the ceremony.

He was old now. Thirty-four years of age. He stood
        there, a larch
A summer – in magic, waiting for the flint axe to fell
        his sap ending.
Much respected, felled with invocations of gratitude at
        the loch.
The old fascination as the ritual progressed, rife

With ecstatic practices. His hair was like raw
        honeycomb
Wrenched from the nest. His tunic draped on his five-
        foot-four frame.
This melancholy he couldn't bear. He could feel his
        chest comb
His skin, trying to break out of the atmosphere above.
        Now lame
In this tough existence of drudgery and early death
        expectancy.
He ached to imagine Naide's face. His bent head
As the willow-to-water's source. Laike lived on
        another year stealthily
Drawn more and more to the increased forests.

And at the years turning, in front of the chamber of
        solstices,
With his children, Laike stood again. A power greater
Than solar systems settled round the spiralled stones.
Outside, Laike closed his eyes. The sun had come up
        again.

Bríd McDonnell

Never

Long curls of justice in the morning,
Smell as sweet as the dying rose...
Long curls of madness in the evening
Taste as bitter as the lemon drops of a pose.

Taste them for me please
Smell them for me please
For I can't smell, nor taste the bitter and the sweet.

Long curls of harshness in the evening
Look as bright as the lights on stage...
Long curls in the night-time
Feel as cold as your humour.

Look at them for me please
Feel them for me please!
For I can't look or feel the bright and the cold.
For life has gone for me
And the crowd will never know me
For I have not made my song after all.

And no, I have fallen

You'll never taste, smell, look and feel me.

Sarah Hopkins

Night Visit

He talked slowly
Not knowing about fast forward
Or narrow attention span

Something about the war years
About queues for bread
Ounces of butter
And tinned marmalade

Suddenly he paused
Eyes locked in time
Scouring a landscape
Once fertile and prime

I need my past, he said,
Unlocking his eyes,
It's my valium of dreams
To meet my tomorrow

If only I could help, sir,
To focus your mind
With advanced technology
Of instant rewind

The nurse at reception
Her smile told a lie
Young ears wrapped in soundscape
To ease her night by.

Gerry Corr

Nineteen Eighty-Five

The old man goes AWOL for once and for all.
On my bedside table, from one end of the year
to the next, a press clipping of Mengele's skull,
a second-hand copy of *L'Etranger* in translation.

Our maths teacher is a big noise in CND.
Somewhere between Easter and the post-exam hoolie
the local paper snaps him in his fallout shelter,
the first of its kind in the twenty-six counties.

There follows a summer of drizzle to break records,
of coaches daily from the square to Ballinspittle,
of leaflets explaining procedure in a four-minute
warning,
of believing the nuclear winter can be sat out

with back issues of *Reader's Digest* and curried beans,
of afternoons rewinding through *When the Wind
Blows*
on a video recorder the size of a dialysis machine
at a time when nobody wonders if it might never.

And little else. Jimmy Hill blubs over Heysel.
Rock Hudson kicks the bucket. September is unsettled.
Mexico City sifts for what's left of itself in rubble.
I make the first of several bids for freedom.

A bit like the wheaten pup a couple of doors down
that chases shadows across the field of a new estate
and isn't seen again despite its owner's weeks of hope
and the ads in shops about it answering to
'Gorbachev'.

There I am - sixteen or so, going on eleven -
thinking myself the last word in a navy Crombie
fetched from the wardrobe of the middle bedroom,
a PLO scarf, a Flock of Seagulls haircut;

smitten with the romance of an umpteenth bomb
on the line in as many days, with my new-found
existential solitude borne of having nobody
- *nobody* - on the platform to wave me off.

Conor O' Callaghan

No Good

Not torturous, not sore.
Not plundered, not lost.
Thundered maybe from my grey cloud,
thrown in from tip to toe top crown.

Watching people, judging,
blaspheming to myself,
an unhappy man.

Camped out in non-sin,
but feeling desolate and impious.
Crying again, but stop, for life,
oh yes, can you feel, just one happiness,
and then, life, life and you, can breathe.
Breathe deeply.

Adrian Neasy

Not To Be

Not to have love returned
To always yearn
She'll ignite your soul
Then watch it burn.

Not to finger her raven hair
As she ascends the stairs
She jokes of 'a few grey hairs'.

Not to nibble her
Slender swan neck
To strike a cord
That creates love.

Not to make her tense
To erect an electric fence
Danger! Don't touch! Beware!
!!!! High Voltage!!!!

Not to live next door
To feel again her pain
Bleeding through damp walls.

Not to be in her heart
As she hurries up Hollow Street
She'll erase you from her soul.

Not to be a prisoner
In the palace of her whims
But commend her
To God's will.

Not to be with her
Is not to be...free
But free to be me
Houdini in her chains.

Patrick Boyle

Ode To A Car Crash

part of the field
it breathes at night
moves a grassy beast
home of grub and worm

victory for wild things
a vision of the future
imagine the driver concussed
thrown from the vehicle

bewildered intoxicated
walking away from the site
the midden now
with a shake of the head

and a dismissive wave of the hand
years later the doors
are rusted unrecognisable
the wheels are gone

but the other driver
shadow driver ghost driver
some days in the night light
you'll find him still

clutching the steering wheel
as if he could take the vehicle
from danger at the crucial last moment
other days he's smoking a cigarette

invisible in the dusty sunshine
as a couple from the city
resettle into the countryside
circling his car's altar

he can never seem to leave it
he has the resigned look of the damned

not that he does not care
for his small cemetery

a caretaker a gardener of sorts
the soil grows the car sinks further
the ants make it home
a scrawny white cat hides from the rain

some days two teenagers kiss
in the back seat
the ghost driver watches shaking his head
but what can he do

the boot is full of old clothes
but nothing goes to waste
one beggar who found the calamity
took himself a coat he still wears today

before long what's in a lifetime
the engine is removed
transplanted to another vehicle
at least part of it

one which swerves its way
around corners in another country
the doors are taken
the seats removed

the glass is spread like fallow seed
its only contribution
to the growth
a glimmer and twitch of light

one day when the surviving driver
turns this bend again he shivers
the car he can't recognise
doesn't see it's submerged

the memory is faint was it here

what turns his blood cold
and pushed his foot
onto the accelerator

is the man standing like a negative
all light on the side of the road
as if he had been waiting
like an old friend

his arm outstretched his thumb hitched
pointing all the way to eternity

Paul Perry

Ode To Nanny
(In memory of my late grand-mother)

The flowering plum blooms in great profusion,
Punctuated by daffodils and narcissi;
And echoes the infinity of your spirit.
For now you are at the source of all things,
That inspirational well of goodness and love.
As your spirit apprehends the Divine;
The Alpha and Omega of Being,
We all comprehend in our individual ways,
Your sublime immersion in God's love,
And your everlasting gaze from above.

Jacqueline Bannon

Omeath

(For the centenary of Patrick Kavanagh's birth)

The soil of Omeath is not grey
But its mud sticks to my feet
Holding me in place.
A bird cannot fly
If it has been doused in petrol fumes
And had its wings clipped by monotony.
My greatest fear is never leaving.

But I've been to the town and it's cold.
Winds are funnelled through the streets.
All stare at the ground
To shield their faces.

And yet I am compelled to go.
I cannot stay
To watch years fly away from me
To sit in an empty pub
Northern accents yelling, "Givvus a pint!"
Recalling things I never did
Because fear compelled me to stay in the mud.
They will not miss me
But I will miss my security blanket
That stole my courage, yet gave me warm comforting
     fear.

Conor Duffy

Omeath Road

Avoid, avoid - interplay of light
Dreams dwell in turmoil, leak through
Bind with tireless divide
Forever circle with madness out of sight
Obscure the mind once more

'Reap the rewards'

Surely the Gods will provide
Never too late!
But why, but why is it so?

I grow weary now, nightmares to sow
Colder now
Leaves bind with time
Face the inevitable decay
The same play is written, same as before
With the sands of time it scatters its seed.

But still I breathe, I smell so much life
God's own delights, such beauty in sight.
Onwards I ride, into the void,
Darkness never far from view
Always on cue.

It is here I shall part
Awaken from the night
Enter the light.

Simon Scott

On Seeing The Autumn Trees in a Lost Friend's Garden

The trees are colourful
And full of beauty
But you are not there
To see.
Their leaves are lingering
Yet,
The sun
Turning to flame
The russet hues,
Inanimate,
They stand
Shrieking their loveliness
To the sky.
These, beloved of you
Are keeping their
Tryst
With the changing
Seasons.
Once upon them
You feasted your eyes
Soaked their loveliness
And gave it back
To us
Enriched with
Some
Of
Your own essence.
Suspended, they await
The final consummation
Already achieved by you,
But the Spring will give them back
Their splendour again,
While we can only
Wonder, about you.

Eileen Johnston

One For The Road

Huddled on O' Connell Street,
Passers by refuse to meet
His gaze. Swarm of legs pass in a haze.

In a bar with smiling faces,
Silly jokes and warm embraces -
Raise a glass and drink to health,
The lucky hand my life has dealt!

Weak from hunger, wet from rain,
Curled up tight, he tries in vain
To sleep. Constant car-horns beep.

Job-promotion celebration,
Moving to a higher station.
Celtic Tiger purred at my door -
No money worries any more.

Comfort is a tattered blanket.
Hugs it tight and humbly thanks
It's welcome heat. His only treat.

A holiday for my kids and wife -
To mark the start of our new life.
Maybe a new car's in order?
After all, can well afford her.

Coins jingle in a plastic cup -
Opens tired eyes, he then looks up:
The stranger's gone. He's hurried on.

Gather round! Drink's on me!
What's wealth without friends and family?
Pour out another! One for the road!
A glorious feeling to get what you're owed.

The highlight of his day has come -

The cup is full, so he buys some
Alcohol, his trusted friend
Will see him through until the end.

Angela Mullen

Outdoors

It happens so easily. We've been watching trees
gather shadow on the wall, on the lookout
for a moment when we might call it a day
and settle for the night. But only our room
is losing ground, while nothing outside is lost.

In the time it takes for him to turn to meet my eye
we have missed it; it has happened without us again.
I give in, put on the light, and watch for him to be
stranded, confronting me from the garden, his back
to me in the kitchen, his eyes in the glass, on me.

What does it matter that we have made a home
where we can draw the curtains and talk of tomorrow,
if we are thinking of this: the shapes we made in
                         darkness,
our kitchen at sea on the lawn, our table set out
in the branches, our faces marooned in stars?

Vona Groarke

Passage Grave

(In memory of Bettina Poeschel)

I go Bettina's way to Newgrange
follow a ridgeline down to the Boyne.
A tomb's mouth in dazzlewhite quartz
swallows the stillness of a winter day.

I join new age pilgrims at a kiosk,
huddled hoods and padded anoraks,
talking of where she was found
over the river near Donore

As rabbits enter a narrow burrow
we squeeze through the passage of stone,
stand in a recessed burial chamber
rising high as a corbelled cone.

We wait in dimness like effigies
I feel the glimmer of the axeman's flint
on ripples, diamonds, spirals, zigzags
picked and pointed on giant slabs.

Bettina never reached Dagda's mound
last resting place of druids and kings.
her killer hid her in a thicket of thorn
a prey to birdlife as she lay alone.

She will not be here at winter solstice
to see the light of the new born sun
creep over the river through frozen fields
flood the tomb in a silver stream.

Maureen Perkins

Peace

As fragile as a wild rose
growing hidden and free,
Down an unfrequented country lane,
Such is peace, delicate, beautiful and gay,
Touch but the petals
and we scatter them all away.

It is the cry of a baby
new born,
heard by a mother
now tired and worn,
Unblemished, untouched,
the world still apart,
A moment divine
Which brings joy to the heart.

A table laid for tea
upon a red checked cloth,
A brown teapot gleaming
in the firelit glow,
Bread baked by patient hands
now eagerly sought,
How peace hovers here
Could we but know.

Peace is,
in the heavy hazy heat
of a summer's day,
The smell of newly cut hay
borne on a balmy breeze,
Barefooted children,
roaming free, untrammelled
              and gay,
Oh weep, for war-weary men
were once such as these.

A red sunset lingers

on a rain washed hill,
The clouds, angry now,
have hidden the sun,
The bereft trees sway
in a disconsolate breeze,
Oh peace, have you fled
these valleys and hills.

Eileen Johnston

Peace Maze

The sun shone through the misty glaze,
As I wandered my way through this special maze,
The sweet, sweet smell of fresh cut grass,
Reminds me of summer, the church and the Mass.
But for this winding path no religion divided,
For both came together, their paths have collided,
To lead to the middle where everyone's led,
And stand side by side to remember the dead.
Millennium new is represented by this,
The reaching hand statue, grasped our dreamed bliss.

So in life we all walk our different ways,
But to one destination, to the end of our days.
At that special time all troubles will melt
Strife is forgotten and each heart truly felt

Eugenia Thompson

Picture

The shed stood, painted white on the roadside,
small and unnoticed but for the foliage
that I could not take my eyes from.
The leaves covering the roof like wet curls
and hanging to the walls with the desperation of ivy.
Of course it was the colour that attracted me,
how leaves creeping bled from tin and stone.
Somewhere off red I stood,
far from blue, my natural home.
We take warmth where we can find it.
And the world moves quickly on,
grey skies offering a soft shower
and in the distance it is fading,
washed away passion in October.

Orla Fay

Pitch and Putt

It's the realm of men
and boys joined in boredom,
the way of life that sees
one day on a par
with the next and school breaks
dragged out too long.

Theirs the hour killed slowly,
the turn for home
in diminishing threes and twos,
the provisional etiquette
of shared tees,
conceded defeat.

Theirs the loose end,
the nationality of ships
in the absence
of shop to talk,
the freedom to be hopeless
and still come back.

Theirs the blather
of the last twoball
accepting flukes
for what they are,
a greenkeeper collecting flags
and shadows in their wake.

Conor O' Callaghan

Queen of Games

If you take a closer look,
What do you think you'll see?
Revealing secrets, deep within
Prove....not all, is as it seems;
And when you lift the shroud that veils,
What do you think you'll find?
This woman stands out, though not alone.
She's just one of her kind.

A queen of mind games,
The scheming sort,
One step ahead of her prey,
A perpetrator of seductive plans,
She knows he'll take the bait;
This mistress of illusion,
So helpless, so naïve;
Oh don't be duped you silly man!
That's her secret to succeed.

She is ambiguous perplexities,
Which you never will conceive,
She executes intricately,
Her plan of hidden perversity.
So dramatic in her temperament,
She makes it seem like art,
So consistent in her persuasions,
This vixen at her craft.

A clever plot of concealed intrigue,
So detailed, yet obscure,
There are very few who can resist,
Her compelling, hypnotic allure;
Many determined by an inner drive,
Try to unlock her mysteries,
Unaware that her evasiveness,
Is a trap of cunning mendacity.

This dominatrix heroine,
So subtle and subdued,
So powerful, yet feminine,
How could any man refuse
Her enticing invitation?
Enchanting fusions of erotic demure,
Guarantees to ensnare fascination,
Caught in her web, there's no escape,
Of this, you can be sure.

What is it of her which captivates?
How does she mesmerize?
Her unassuming eloquence?
Or the elegance of her smile?
You presume to out-smart her agenda,
A warning word to the wise,
Stay alert if you wish to befriend her,
And never be fooled by her guise.

Her innovative strategies,
Those methods of delusion,
That integrated complexity,
Precedes the inevitable conclusion.
Her goal achieved, anything she wants received
Should come as no surprise,
With an essence of beguiling overtures,
She gazes into his eyes.

Welcome to my parlour,
Mused...the spider about her fly.

Clare Ana Lalor-Fitzpatrick

Real Fiction

Been scheming my schemes,
I've been dreaming my dreams,
Been thinking these thoughts that remind me of you.
I don't need a reason –
It's psycho-hunt season,
Discover a world where nobody's true.
There's the good and the bad,
The guilty, the sad,
And we all have to pay for our crime,
There's always a fight;
It's tough being right
And I feel like I'm wasting my time.
By the time I get near
You'll have all disappeared;
I trust in a twist of the knife,
But it's all just the same,
To you it's a game,
It's a game that you've played all your life.
My blade shining bright:
I'm a thief in the night
And your soul is what I've come to steal;
The sorrow, the pain,
The sting of the rain,
Who said this was part of the deal?
Torn up at the roots
I'm just jumping through hoops
As I dance like a puppet on strings,
Even monsters need names,
I'm a lion being tamed,
For your rod I no longer have wings.
Blood's all you lack
When you're stabbed in the back,
They say that true friendship is rare.
But I live without fear
And I'll always be here,
I guess nobody said life was fair.

Kathryn Lambe

161

Rebirth

Anne's* child was born,
And you held Medbh in your arms
Before your time of death, Therese.*
We were in despair after you.

Whilst you lived your vulnerable
Emotions surfaced, only then
Did I feel your angelic presence
I could not stop calling you darling
With your dainty ways you made us love you.
You died in early spring,
We were thrown into confusion.
The beginning of your new life
Had just begun in your letting go.

You were too beautiful to live too long
In this life with our thronging masses

And if you journey too far ahead of us
In the celestial realms, if when I die
I cannot reach you, cannot find you
In the crowded heavens still
All of us would be inseparable
At one with the family of man in God.

And we would find you there.

Bríd McDonnell

* *Anne and Therese, both sisters of the poet – Ed.*

Red Rose

Scarlet lady
once jostling
for the limelight,
where is your bloom?

Tight budded,
heavy scented,
on ball gown breast,
you danced till dawn.

Now overblown
lady of the night
gown tattered,
moonface shattered,

thorns jag
your wilted neck.

Maureen Perkins

Reflection

With thanks dear God
For the hope you have shown me
And for the heartaches
For without them I would not
Know love, nor how to show it.

With praise dear God
For the joys you have brought me
And the sadness
For without them I would not
Know joy or how to recognise it.

With love dear God
For the spirit you have taught me
And the spiritlessness
For without them, I would not
Know spirit or how to receive it.

Jessica Coyle

Remembrance of a Forgotten Mother

The sitting ducks on a lake
Quiet water stirring gently.
Rushes soothing in the wind,
whistling softly like a still bird.
Water as sweet as that lake,
pure and good and true,
can sometimes in one instant be
torn and killed and gone.
Shivering quivers of smoke burned bridges
and forlorn families cry in vain.
With pain, follows grief
In every which way.

Music of our senses
deafen our souls, plundering
hearts are trampled.
The two foot boy
who drowned
in the two foot river.
Crying forever in his mother's heart,
torn wasted womb, but heart of
pure joy and gold.

The things that happen
I persist, are neither good nor bad.
They are dreams we had,
our voices short and tapping
on the door of life.
She died with little happiness, no smile.
Yet I will always smile for her,
my blood, enriched with hers,
I cry for you....

Adrian Neasy

Revelation

My concepts were always so dogmatic, so foolproof
until we met.
I remember the conversations whispered tamely in our
microcosmic corner
Of the world. You shine now, brilliantly, in the neon
spheres. Tell me, Grace,*
Is it that we all hold part of the truth? Will you tell me
now.

If I were you and you were me, and he was she and she
was he. Revelation.
With many lives lived, we learn on in quiet wonder,
with humanity.
Our souls, like birds to morning, ever rise to God.
It is as if we are all so intrinsically as one, so close to
one another
That we are everyone that ever was on this earth and
that ever will be.

And time is all we have left to love.

Bríd McDonnell

*Grace was friend of the poet, a person of another
faith – Ed.*

166

Rhythm of Life

Ebb and flow of blood to the heart
Beats with the rhythm
Of the pulse of man

In the centre of life
Silent and awake
Mystical heart waits

Beating with the rhythm of
The pulse of Christ.

Fears, hopes
Grief and sin
And all of human love
Absorbed by him
And in the silence of his heart returned
Leaping up to life
Life blood of Christ flows
I in him and
He in me.

Mary Lisetta

Roisin O'Rue

Now Katie chased her from the sky
As she poisoned snakes who caught her eye
So across Thunder River she quickly withdrew
There to look for widows and sorrow them with brew
And always left the way she came
Gatherin' curses to her name
The she spread purple to disease
And brought heroics to its knees
But oh so hideous she was
A branch of lightening had to pause
She did slander goose and gander
Hide evil in an eye
Bewitch the Galway salmon
And fishermen who lie
Caw-sars* from the chimney fled
Screamin' nightmares left their bed
The hen was out before cock crew
Hiding where her wings were due
Even death had left his stolen breath
The state of graveyards was a fret
Ghosts move about in torn dresses
The odd had coffins with addresses
From fiery smoke came a shriek and yell
Was some witch and ghoul creatin' hell
Sprang Hip McKeon who grabbed a bone
And after death he went
He snapped his scythe by which he died
And broke his heart of flint
Poor Annie Crust had left the dust
With just a nail or two
But she gave his eye to a sad magpie
Before the hangman knew
Death said to grieve his faithful wife
Again they tried to take my life
Sure there's not one left to fear my name
Sew an oul' habit to cover my shame
As I've lost account among the dead

And grief there's not a tear to shed
I shall take some rest amid this gloom
At least I'll fill an empty tomb
Stormin' trees in the woods of groan
Found many roots were not their own
From snowy pass to Lilac Glen
Spring was late and dreamt again
Then nothin' was as it were known
The oul moop- mo** left pigeon's moan.

*crows
** ancient word for pigeon - Ed

(From 'Seaneen and the Goblins')

Pat Bennett

Save Us From War

How loving
How joyous
Are children everywhere!
How innocent
Are babies everywhere!

Wars are not declared
By the children.
Guns are not aimed
By babes.

Boundaries are claimed
Troop movement planned
Cities are levelled
Farmlands destroyed
By men who once
Were children
By women who once
Were babes.

Ah, Children! Dear children!
You can save us from war!

As you are growing
Hold fast that
Innocence
Wherewith you were clothed.
Never cease loving!
Guard each bit of
Your joy!

Bombs are not
Devised by the innocent.
Polemics do not come
From the lips of the loving.
Cruelty and joy
Do not mingle.

Dear children!
Stay loving
Stay joyous
Stay innocent.

And you'll save us from war!

Adrian Saich

Say My Friend

Say my friend that memory is longer than this day,
this full day of my life,
that in the night as I sleep time away
I am not lost.

Say my friend that I am the moon
when the sun has set in the western sky,
that I am alive in your dreams
and part of the tears that you cry.

Say my friend that you believe in ghosts
when shadows move across the earth,
that somehow past and present will entwine
in the steady beating heart.

Say my friend that love is strong and true
when beaten down by time,
that when your lips are blue and cold
the warm kisses you remember will be mine

Say my friend that night and day
cannot be parted long,
that one day soon dawn will break
And forever we will be one.

Orla Fay

Seasons

The silence of the sunny Sunday morning
Is lightly broken
By the happy sound of children playing
Adding to the tranquillity
That my garden and I share.

Nelly Moser smiles shaking her pink face
In the light breeze
Head held high in the spring of life
Looking down upon the fading rhododendron bloom
With a superiority of youth.

The bloom of the camellia is gone
Moved to a new stage of life
The changing seasons appear in an instant
Before my eyes
I see life's path played out in bloom.

Nelly Moser, there is no need to be smug
A procession of buds
Yet to blossom await their turn
To take the place of those flourishing
Beautiful blooms
In a flash winter will arrive
And all will be gone.

Cyril Nolan

Seatown

Sanctuary of sorts for the herons all day yesterday
waiting for the estuary to drain and this evening
for two lights queuing like crystal at the top of the bay.

Last straw for the panel beaters only just closed down
and the dole office next to the barracks and the gold
of beer spilled on the pavements of Saturday
                    afternoon.

Home from home for the likes of us and foreign boats
and groups with oilskins and unheard-of currencies
in search of common ground and teenage prostitutes.

Reclaimed ward of bins left out a week and dogs in
                    heat
and the fragrance of salt and sewage that bleeds
into our garden from the neap-tide of an August night.

Poor man's Latin Quarter of stevedores and an early
                    house
and three huge silos swamped by the small hours
and the buzz of joyriders quite close on the bypass.

Time of life to settle for making a fist of love
and glimpsing new dawns and being caught again
and waking in waves with all the sheets kicked off.

Point of no return for the cattle feed on the wharves
and the old shoreline and the windmill without sail
and time that keeps for no one, least of all ourselves.

May its name be said for as long as it could matter.
Or, failing that, for as long as it takes to the pilot
to negotiate the eight kilometres from this to open
                    water.

Conor O' Callaghan

174

Silenced Memory

With so much expression preceding, I find myself
mystified,
A struggle it seems, to put your mind at ease.
But this is a heart that, when it comes to you, will
never accept defeat.
Knowing of my desire to prove my love to you,
With a genuine devotion, driven by boundless
determination to make you believe,
Once again, I give to you, my words...

I want you to know that missing your smile would be
like closing my eyes to each beautiful sunrise,
Breaking forever free from your embrace would
release me from the one place I feel safe in this life,
Not having your eyes to escape to, would take from
me, the doorway to heaven,
And losing contact with your mind would mean letting
go, the insight of an angel.
You are the sweet divine sunshine breathing life to
every element exquisite in this life of mine,
Your beauty unbelievable, undeniable, inconceivable,
so reliable,
And you continue to be the first thought of my day,
last at night and every thought in between.

I will never let you go from this life,
I will never say goodbye,
And you will never become...
....a silenced memory.

Raymond Boileau

Silversmith

The rounded moon sits pale on a January afternoon
humbled by the sun, eerily coexisting
in the sky, beyond the horizon is science fiction.

Yesterday a watered down sun spilt across paper
that was a golden ocean
in a moment of absorption.

On some smithy the hammer hits the anvil,
tap, tap, tap ringing through the evening
but what is made is intangible yet.

It is a paper moon today.

Letters are silver by moonlight,
cold, clear and pure.

A word is a key for every lock,
for every question posed by the sun
there is a dreamy moon.

Thought is an alchemy turning gold to silver.

Orla Fay

Snow At Tara Hill

The Mound of the Hostages
Meets my eye;
The surrounding landscape
Adorned with snow,
The legacy of the ancients
Confronts my gaze,
As I witness the jewels
Of Celtic craftsmanship.

The valley below is draped in white;
The panoramic winter view
Suffused in light,
This site is testament to Celtic might,
A distillation of civilization.

Jacqueline Bannon

Snow On The Mountains

Several giant steps away
the Dublin mountains
are a ripple
of watercolour blues.

Crested with landslides of snow
in the widescreen
of my mind.

A cartoon of skiers
flashes of red, yellow, blue
toboggan downwards.

Weaving like skaters
laughing like children.

Thomas Clarke

So Much More Than Words
Can Ever Hold

With each golden sunrise on a fresh day to
Deep into the night when the moon hangs high above
              the world
I think of you and my heart smiles.
I could travel the whole world over
But I would never find a love like yours again
A love only a father and daughter could know.
A love that goes beyond what I can say.
I came into a world where I was a secret, where no one
              could ever know me
Where love's arms didn't hold me
Until you came along so selflessly and chose me as
              your daughter.
You loved me unconditionally, endlessly, truly.
You breathed life into my veins
You gave me the words that shaped my voice
You made me with love and patience, discipline and
              tears
Then bit by bit stepped back to release me
Allowing me to sail upon my sea
You are the very spirit within mine
The generous soul of nature,
The wisdom of the ages,
The power of the eagle's flight,
The patience of eternity,
The depth of a family need
I want you to know I love you so very much
So much more than words can ever hold.

Lynn Dowling

179

Soham Angels, Holly and Jessica

On Sunday, August 4th, 2002,
A family in Soham had a barbecue.
Two beautiful friends were there on the day,
Holly and Jessica loved to play.

They stood in the kitchen for a photograph,
Then went upstairs to have a laugh.
Later in the evening as night did fall,
Holly's mum, Nicola, gave them a call.

On approaching Holly's bedroom, inside it was bare,
Clothes on the bed were all that were there.
Alarm bells went off which gave out a fright,
Where could Holly and Jessica be on that night?

Friends and family covered miles and miles,
Searching for two girls and their beautiful smiles.
Sadly two weeks later their search did end,
When Holly's body was found and Jessica her friend.

Cambridgeshire grew silent, the town had died,
Their sadness and tears they couldn't hide.
Two Angels were taken away from their town,
No doubt in heaven looking down.

We talk to the Angels up above,
To send Holly and Jessica all our love.
We'll remember both deep in our hearts.
On the day Holly and Jessica did depart.

Mummy and Daddy love you so,
But there's no hurry in letting you go.
You brought us sunshine every day,
Holly and Jessica you're special in every way.

At night when the stars are in the sky,
We think of you both and start to cry.

But if you see a falling star,
It's a sign from two angels wherever you are.

When we look back on the fun times we had,
Those fun times now make us so sad.
Your family and friends send you their love,
Picturing Holly and Jessica as Two White Doves.

So goodnight two princesses, we love you so much,
We'll talk to the angels to keep in touch.
We'll tuck you in on your bed of cloud,
Holly and Jessica, You made us so proud!

Larissa Reilly

Sophie's (Toscan Du Plantier's) Last Moments

The earth is cold beneath me
I scratch, it will not give
The night
Bears down above me
It wears an ugly grin

Cold, ice cold
Earth's grit beneath my teeth
A sticky blindness imprisons
Shattered fragments
Of my skull

Leaden limbs enwrapped
'Tis a thorny bed
Of nettled down
Entangling me
In a briary shroud.

A distant muffled
Animal sound
Smothered
In the moonless night
A light beckons

Unimpeded flight
I soar above this carcass
It draws me back against my will
A light goes out.

The shadow stays behind.

Bernadette Martin

Sorrows Eye

Let the sun chase shadows
from the valley's green
and the flowers display
what God wants seen

As again we think of days
gone by
for the heart alone
has sorrows eyes

Yet joy has left the fragrance
of its breath
that's much too sweet
to lie in death.

Pat Bennett

Sorrows of Adam

I still set a table for those who're not here
'Twas a place for livin' endowed with much cheer
Since the door closed with sorrow I watch for the post
They were once, are they now, or gone like a ghost
I am left with some thoughts which are pictures of
when
But I'm livin' and thinkin' and dyin' in them.

They shall come to this table oft' wet by a tear
And think of the one that sorrow left here
I shall wish to be with them, but as now shall they
know
As they walk to a pace of those long ago
For in all the fine thoughts which love sprinkled then
They shall be livin' and thinkin' and dyin' in them.

Shall they call on the one to still what they fear?
Trust in the mercy for which he came here
Surge with his hope through this ocean of moan
Way that he is to gather his own
The sorrows of Adam come to all men
To be livin' and thinkin' and dyin' in them.

Pat Bennett

Sparkling Treasures;

As the blueness fills my eyes, sun rising in the sky,
I think of my dear childhood,
The days that have gone by;
The memories I have locked inside
Are shared with just a few.
If only I could bring them back,
To make them all brand new.

The border town protected me and I loved it back,
The old style streets and rich night air,
It never seemed to lack,
So then we never saw our streets;
We went our different ways,
Our hopes and dreams fulfilled and lost,
The passing of the days.
We look ahead, our heads held high,
To see another bright blue sky,
Until that day that my eyes feel,
The sparkle of the blueness real.

Eugenia Thompson

Spring Clearing

But for the rain
I'd have cut you down
That first evening.
Your flailing body
Floundered awkwardly
As beech and oak
Stood shoulder to shoulder
Mocking.

Shapeless and gaunt
A few leaves curled
Dry and colourless
At your feet.
No chance of flower
Or blood red berry
Would redeem you from
A deserved fate
Now.

When I return
The next day
A mossy cup
Twined in blue
Snoozes securely
In your boughs.
You have made your point.
Summer will come
After all.

Máire Larney

Squandered Life

Days are going so fast
Beads of a rosary
Carelessly said and
Finished before properly begun
Swiftly the hours pass through my fingers
Meaningless unless given to You

What depth of feeling rises
Wavers in the air
And disappears!
Fierce colours of passion
Bright hues of love
Dark purple of despair
Grass that springs up in morning
Cast into the furnace at night
Sadness of lost childhood years
Happy days forgotten in
Life's struggle for existence

The world moans
And sadder still
Is unknowing that it moans
Desperate people twisted
Into plastic shapes
With plastic smiles
Despairing of love
Compromise with pleasure, power or pity
All of human misery -
The hungry, the tortured, the oppressed -

Yet still the spark of life is there
A smile, a kindly word
The lifting of the heart
In a moment of grace.
Lord, I could love them all!
But I am too in pain -
I cannot spare myself to give to them

And so I give to You.
Not them but us.
Into your caring heart I give
My care for them
And all my sad desires
You will use my love
Although polluted
And transforming it give back
What I alone could not
Streams of living water
Poured out for us and
Saving us from death.

Mary Lisetta

Stardust

Just a little bit of stardust
That's all you've ever been
In this vast expansive landscape
For fifteen billion years

Oceans deep and mountains high
Your scale is what you see
Your breath is like the wind that blows
On calm and choppy seas

Your spirit is the dawning day
That whistles in the wind
Your tears torrential droplets
Washing down the trees

Your shape is like an old oak tree
Shaking boughs for birds and bees
Your folding arms are like the night
As dusk descends and peters out

Your floor and roof, the ozone layer
Galaxies, your friends at play
You've sauntered on the milky way
A shining light calls all to prayer.

Bernadette Martin

Starlight

Wild, wild was the day that sent us weeping, running
across the strand
At Blackrock, where we once dared the waves. Where
the bands
Played frolics to the sound of the trumpets of a once
Forgotten Troy. Wild, wild was the wind that sent us,
all at once

Scattered across the townlands of Louth and beyond,
Our childhood innocence swamped in the offerings of
the pond
At Ladywell. Wild, wild is the night where we have
come
Suppliant, weighed down with the problems, not just
some,

Of our nuclear age. And when we were always
travelling
There was a star somewhere in the night sky. The land
is parching
Now, oh mother, mother earth. Where is the berth
Where we can scramble onto? Come into our aching
birth

And bless us with chrism. And when I go back, when I
go back
To never-ever land, on those Mesolithic beaches of
once there was
Upon a time. And I will remember. Wild, wild is the
sunshine
Upon the beach now. Let all who stood find being.
Please will you shine
On, Star of Bethlehem, shine on.

Bríd McDonnell

Sugar Rose

Summer blossoms sugar rose as tiger lilies bloom,
My eyes are graced by the beautiful scenery, that is
beautiful you.
An excited air of love descends as you dance among
the winds,
If it were wrong to gaze upon your spirit, I would
gladly sin
Your enchanting presence seizes my eye as every day is
born
With such magnificence, the world I know will never
be lovelorn
Until time fades and memories follow, I'll know that
one thing was true
That you were selflessly beautiful, selflessly you.

Raymond Boileau

Sunlight

It is on the black back of a crow,
makes the leaves on a tree shimmer,
(from a distance the tree runs like water).
It fills and shadows the sky,
alters the face of the land.
Light is everywhere;
falling on the kitchen table,
onto wood, onto paper,
comes into my eyes, makes me warmer.

(This is a song for the fallen angel
following the sun into the west)

Remember the trail of primroses, daffodils,
daisies, buttercups, dandelions, bluebells,
cowslips and wild roses.
Remember the smell of sweet pea
and the taste of parsley.
Remember your feet and the earth.

The day gets longer at the end of February.
I cannot escape that this is Ash Wednesday
and the psyche is indelibly marked
as the black ash rubbed on a forehead.

Pagan light still whitens the crow,
sees a tree as a waterfall flow
into a shrine,
follows Christ into the sunset,
golden, heavenly sunlight.

Orla Fay

Sunrise

*"See sunrise and sunset,
and nothing but dreams between."*   - *John Ruskin*

The February morning is damp with mist,
the fields covered in frost, the air chilled,
falling and tumbling.

The trees are dark and solid in stark contrast.
There is a whiteness in the sky lifting
and grey clouds that smudge the sky like ink on paper.

Frost is creeping to the throats of daffodils,
the grass like chalk, the sky becoming powder blue.
The sun is rising like a lemon in the East.

And now the sun is bleeding into the powder blue.
I don't know why but it is a treat,
like raspberry and blackberry mixed together.

The sky becomes rippled with gently moving cloud.
Suddenly I'm falling into a river of amber,
tumbling into the centre of the sun.

It is so close and so far away, a piece of heaven,
                        sunrise,
I cannot wear these colours, they are too fleeting.

I'd like to take photographs...

They wouldn't do...

If I could pause and take a still...

Zoom in at an angle...

Do you see?

Do you see?

Wish you could....

Orla Fay

Tainted Angel

I am that angel
Winged as thee.
Floating high above the sky
But yet I feel great pain.

Caught in love's fine trap.
White as whitest sand,
I was tainted by love's red hand,
Scalding me with venom.

Poisoned and hurt
I tried to fly away,
But my wings broke.
Love hurts.

Edged rings of flames
Burn my soul inside.
Spreading from heart to soul
I try to subside.

This tainted love I felt
Left behind me.
Ridiculous thoughts ridicule me.
Can love ever be real?

Adrian Neasy

Tattered Tears

War, Power, Allies, NATO
boom from the radio,
sitting on the seat
beside my mother.

I watch her -
tears in her eyes
as she makes the evening meal
from meagre morsels,
compliments of the West.

She watches the sky,
fear furtively
furrowing features,
eyes sad, unsmiling.

She picks up the picture
of Father,
its frame, fragmented,
long dead, gone,
compliments of War.

Bombs, smoke, cries -
boom from the street,
as I sit on the seat
beside my mother.

I cradle her bloodied face
against my chest.
The frame, now free
slips slowly to the floor.
Smiling sighs from silent lips,
the quiet tears, no more.

Verna Keogh

Tea Leaves

I hope it was no lie I bought today
She stirred the tealeaves then I heard her say
Your lover will return from far away
She claimed a token of me for good measure
A token? Small exchange for such a treasure.

I fear it was a lie I bought today

For to the next who came I heard her say
Your lover will return from far away
I did not grudge the gypsy girl a token
Within her eyes I glimpsed her own heart broken.

Adrian Saich

The Ancient Grief

There is an ancient grief
sitting deep inside my bones.

It is older
than the wounds of personal history.
older
than the so called trauma of birth.

This ancient grief
remembers death.

It remembers appearances.
And more poignantly,
it remembers
the disappearance of things.

The Great Mystery
is that things are.

That each thing
is a presentation
from the shadows.

And the ancient grief?

It is like a soft echo
heard
underneath the surface of things.

All that appears
is twinned
to what will disappear.

Kalichi

The Ballad of Linda

Linda lived her life alone
Shunning the common herd
Her heart entombed with some old grief
Of which she spoke no word.

For two and forty years she moved
A challenge to the town
With head a trifle high she passed
The gossips up and down.

In subtle ways they tried to trace
A scandal to her door
But failing they would loose their tongues
And scarlet sin deplore.

Once April snow lay on the ground
Could they believe their eyes!
Footprints led straight to her back door
And they were full man-size.

Just why this visitor had come
Only Linda knew
And only she knew why she came
Herself at twenty-two

Gently holding in her arms
A frail new baby girl
With eyes as wistful as her own
And cheeks as white as pearl.

Linda faced their searing scorn
Bearing it like a queen
With all the surface of her life
Unbroken and serene.

They did not sheathe their serpent fangs
When Linda's baby died

They spoke no word of tenderness
Instead they crucified.

With hearts as hard as cobblestones
They flayed her through the years
In prideful poverty she lived
Scorning need of tears.

Then suddenly Linda died
The neighbours laid her out
Upon an open coffin
The custom thereabout.

Still all their muted whisperings
Were bare of sympathy
At last perhaps they might unveil
Linda's mystery.

For pinned above her worn-out heart
Upon her old chemise
A locket held a miniature
And two thin silver Keys.

They knew the keys would surely fit
Linda's cedar-box
They poorly hid their eagerness
To be about the locks.

I left....I had no wish to see
The desecration start
Their ruthless curiosity
Might wake her pulseless heart.

Had I known I would have stayed
To smile at their dismay
To box was empty...God stood guard
Where vandals pried that day...

Adrian Saich

The Book

Inside each of us
is a sacred book
in it we were meant to look
but the cover is rarely lifted.

Or pages rarely cut
as we are taught to find all
we are told we need
in society's creed.

A creed
that cannot feed
the searching soul
cannot make you whole
or reach your perfect goal.

Instead we play a role
endlessly
wishing we were free.

Thomas Clarke

The Brightening
(On making a new friend)

Outside the window
Someone cared to stop and look
And as she looked
Shadows turned to substance
Outlines were defined and
Colours glowed
Others were passers-by
They missed
The window brightening
Reflecting back the love
That gave to the self the self.

Mary Kearns

The Candlelight Coast

Come soft blue night, come summer rain
to fall and speckle the windowpane
of a starry world.
Candlelight quiver to raindrop stars
caught in a web of threaded silver.
Smattering commune with quiet earth
and drink down deep the brimming heart.
Silently go to the ground
where streams are lost
and peace is found.
And dwell all night in blue and silver,
in rain and earth as lights go out
across the countryside.
Sleep and dream to dream and sleep
to rest and know a voice of rain
blesses the earth with a smattering.
As lights go out across the countryside
from the city
to the sea lost in memory
remember the voice
of the rain saying
quite nothing at all
but that it sounded
like a quiet heart.
Still in the night
some ships are sailing
like dreams put out to sea.
They go to meet a voice,
a voice of rain
long after my curtain is drawn
they go to meet a dawn
after midnight
and some time
of hours past
sailing by the window.
Like dreams they go,
like dreams they go

up along the candlelight coast
of another country.

Orla Fay

The Dancing Deck at Boggan Cross

On a Summer's Sunday evening in nineteen-thirty-
three,
The Dancing Deck at Boggan Cross was the place to
be,
To see the crowds that gathered there,
And dance the night away.

Times were hard and money scarce,
No one came by car,
They all came on their bicycles,
Some with partner on the bar.

They danced half sets and waltzes,
Quicksteps and Foxtrots too,
The Walls of Limerick, Siege of Ennis,
They all danced them too.

James Casey called the dances,
He was the MC,
There was no charge back then,
Admission? It was free.

There were two grand musicians,
Cormeen two man band,
Petie O' Brien - a fiddler of repute,
John Matthews, mandolin and flute.

They played such lovely music,
It was a treat to hear,
Just to sit there listening,
It was so easy on the ear.

They came from Muff and Kingscourt,
K'Wood and Nobber too,
Moynalty and from Mullagh
And some from Bailieboro' too.

The dances finished at eleven,
That was the law back then,
And as they grabbed their bikes for home,
To be back that night week again.

William O' Brien

The Dry Ship 'Dollo'

(For my brother Gregory)

We left the pool of Dundalk town,
To sail for New York Bay;
With all the hatches battened down,
The paint and brightwork gay.

Tall lofty sails billow full,
The shrouds tuned new and tight;
And purpoise-fast, the leak-proof hull,
Bound forward day and night.

With Biscay Bay astern us now,
And Spain port-side East;
Foam bubbles 'round the surging bow,
Like yearned-for beery yeast.

Then Westing South, towards the Isles,
That make Madeira, a wine-soaked halt,
I think of wines' nostalgic smiles,
But all I taste is salt.

Still south, we go, a-westing,
With Canaries' brandy well abeam;
With sailors nerves a-testing,
It's rum, oh rum, we dream.

The broiling Sun, the waters' splash,
Brings on a dreadful thirst;
A man could kill, spend all his cash,
And drink till he would burst.

On, and on, the straining ship,
Turns west on its long run.
Men work like demons, to speed the trip,
And get the dry voyage done.

With liquid thoughts, with craving wants,

With nerves like violin strings,
Men drive the ship, until she pants -
It's really rage that sings.

Oh whisky, gin, and golden ale,
As flying fish skim past:
Bermuda lies behind our tail,
New York's before the mast.

The Hudson's beacons guide like stars,
 - New York's a million bottles bright -
Throw down the gangplank, find the bars,
'Good men, we'll drink tonight'.

We'll drink it large; we'll drink it small,
We'll quaff a merry sup;
And when we've drained the taverns all,
We'll drink the Hudson up.

Nicholas Kearns

The Farewell

Stuck in ruts of decaying dreams,
flapping with birds extinct and gone,
died off and suffered and it seems
I fluttered down to death.
Rested and lifefilled for a change,
its time for a simple farewell.
The double-bass = dung, dung dung-pluck,
piano keys, nodding heads and lazy arm.
Music so soft and soothing, causing no harm
to one's heart, the tears of joy
are noisy down my cheek, wanting them
to look real at my farewell,
I pleaded
Bleeded anguish, seeping pus out of my eyes.
Just leave in the end. Thank you!
The last piano note rolled out,
vicious and angry for my waste and ridicule.
I slammed the lid shut,
Tight and Tight.

Adrian Neasy

The Gate To Mulcahy's Farm

The gate to Mulcahy's farm is crooked,
sinking into infirm soil like a ship
from the Spanish Armada if you like,
forged and felled in some dark cave

to find itself jaded with flaking eroded gilt
leaving the striations prison-like,
shaded a coppery green. A gate without
a handle and unlike all others in any

neighbouring field without the dull sanguine
frame that swings to and fro like a hinge,
or a door itself to some other world.
No, this is no ordinary gate and there is

something majestic in its stolid refusal
to swing, something absurd even.
Perhaps this is another version of heaven,
imagine the bedroom it might once have graced,

this brass headboard, this discarded,
transported remnant of love's playground,
and look, two golden and intact globes
rest on either end, both transcendental
transmitters,

receivers maybe of rough magic,
piebald love, communicating not sleep,
sleep no more, but wake, wake here
to the earth and imagine if you want

the journey of such an armature
of fecund passion, what hands gripped
these bars, what prayers were murmured
through the grate of this ribald cagery?

Imagine too the man who must have

hurled and pitched and stabbed
this frame into the ground, in a dark rain of course
after his wife had died, her passing to us unknown

though you know this
that there must have been some act
of violence within this frame-work,
some awful, regrettable pattern caught

in the form of what? Wind rushing through a brass
headboard, an exclamation point to the querulous
division of fields, could we be talking border-country,
and the broken, airy, moss-eaten stone walls.

Think about when the farmer died and the farm
was sold, think about what happened, the field,
empty of its cows, still with its stones and grey soil,
maybe this is Monaghan,

maybe some day, the brass headboard
you are looking at now, will be sold
to an antiquarian in a Dublin shop,
brought there on a traveller's horse and cart,

not smelted down or disassembled, but sold
to a store where some lady with a wallet
will buy the thing, the elegant shabbery before you
that is the gate to Mulcahy's farm. As for the bed

itself, we can speculate, let it have sunken
into the earth, or better still let the earth be the bed,
the cot, the mattress and berth to this sinking
headboard,
this beautiful incongruous reliquary of misplaced
passion.

Paul Perry

The Growing Place

This is my land
that stretches and falls back
like a yawn or a long shadow.

My soil is brown and darkened
ploughed in ridges running
to meet a horizon of ditches.

My trees are tall and elegant
awakening their senses
with fresh foliage

breathing the clean air,
moisture laden
and sun kissed.

The churches call
through the villages,
their spires are pillars,

their bells my civilisation,
my childhood Jesus,
my lost confession.

But my God is
the flowers,
the snowdrops and daffodils,

the sunlight on my cheek,
the lengthening evening,
the promise of summer.

I am at once
beneath the soil,
the root subconscious.

I was born before

the idea was formed
before the word had lips.

My land, my soil, my trees,
my God, my flowers,
my sunlight imagined

somewhere years ago, unborn,
as I slept, somewhere universal
as the heart is, a growing place...

Orla Fay

The Knock

That sudden knock upon my door
granddad welcomes granny
we date and drive, drink, dine, dance,
while children. listening in our blood
remember this.

Brendan Connolly

The Land of Eagles

When you sing and your voice wavers
it is the emotion that you cannot contain
and I think that you know the weight of your words
because they fall like a burden,
d
r
o
p
to the place where tears are made
and spread out boldly and loudly
until I think of wings unfolding,
of eagles and angels and heaven.

How quick the progression from
brown to golden to white.
When you sing you are your human best
though the quiver in your voice
is the pitfall of your potential,
b
r
e
a
k,
it makes you beautiful.

So this is the land of eagles then,
the place where tears are made
but I do not know how to cry
I only know how to smile
s
o
a
r
through the heartland.

Orla Fay

The Lighthouse

I heard her tell the story another way.
She set it, not in the village, where
the parish priest was telling the crowd
about light in the darkness
and the dawn of a new age -

she set it in the kitchen of their house,
with three women resting
and the day's work done. She told it
so we would listen for the music
of the room when it was still:

the rustle of the fire in the grate;
the single note of a teaspoon
from which the knitting needles took their cue;
the steady flutter of the carriage clock
that kept their breath in check.

One of them might sleep and her nodding glasses
snag the firelight and scatter it
around the room to return in the more
familiar shine of cups on the dresser,
copper pans, her sister's wedding band.

In the village, a crowd of overcoated men
sent up a cheer for progress and prosperity
                    for all...

And in the length of time
it took to turn a switch and to make light
of their house, three women saw themselves

stranded in a room that was nothing like
their own, with pockmarked walls
and ceiling stains, its cobwebs and its grime:
their house undone and silenced
by the clamour of new light.

Vona Groarke

The Pin Fastener

Down through the layers of peat you lay
Waiting to be discovered, damp, you sought
To preserve the memory of those early iron-age
Hands who fondled you, until she cried

And cried at battle-ending. You had held her cloak
In position when the wind was wild and rain
Lashed relentlessly on their Dun. Or on warmer days
With the women grinding corn or weaving the revered
                    cloth

Of the chief. The sacred books hadn't been written.
                    They gathered you,
Threw you in the lake with other treasures, a votive
                    offering
To Lughaidh. Consolidating his benevolence, you
Stayed for over two thousand years until we came
                    crunching

Across the dried lake bed. Now I hold you delicately
In my hands, feeling your smoothness as the hands
                    that held you
So long ago. Suddenly there is no time
But the one time, and the Deity is come

To bless. Objects never change as we do, in our way
Of existence, perishable. But you, little dress-fastener,
                    remind
Of the millennia where nobody quite died. Were only
Transferred to another existence. And the land

Lies drowsy with our ancestors' bones as we move on
Across the pained peaks
Of our evolution.

Bríd McDonnell

217

The Rescued

You hold tightly to your
White body a blanket of houses
To keep away the memory of too
Little for too many
Your quilt is poor armour because the
Scar of not enough is deeply ingrained
On your weakened heart
You carry other wounds of
Lands and birthrights lost and stolen
A bloodline of resentment
A family folklore of who not to trust
Tenderly passed on to the
Next

I have an interest in our Incredible Next
I oversee with unfathomable love
The rise of the shivery sun on his day and
The rise of the moon on his dreamless night
He is Incredible, our Next
He who can guide a warring two to
Be Friends
This Incredible Next will be strong
Enough for the binds of his history
I will wrap him with the armour
Of my love so that he will be
Sufficient warrior not to battle.
You hold tightly to your
White body a blanket of houses
Your Next stands lance in hand
Carrying your colours, flying your flag
Each the other's champion
With the woman a distant vessel
Brimming over with her unfathomable love.

Margaret McCooey

The Ring

They have married our bones
the first ones live within
hammocked in our hearts
they hunger still
one day, one life, one love.

Brendan Connolly

The Shadow

Because I do not know you
Other than intimately
So that in you
I see myself
Alike, and opposite
Imagined, and real
You inhabit the electric
Signals in my pulse.

Nude, I wear you
Dressed, my skeleton
Hangs in your wardrobe
Dangling its admonitions
When the time comes
I will shed you
Like a life-long habit
And enter into another.

Peter Murphy

The Stick Harvest
(For Benny)

Shortly after the winter solstice
I saw you hurry down the road,
cycling with head down in approval
of the fullness of this fruitfall,
bicycle aching with the stick-harvest.

As you moved, bushes rose to cover you.
Gateway dipped to reveal you and your bundle
crossing the Bridge disappearing from view.
Heading home, mornings work done,
glinting off your handlebars the new sun.

John Noonan

The Stuff

I, John Mouse, Dot Com,
Do solemnly attest and firmly hold
After a diligent enquiry into stuff,
So witness to the whereabouts of same.

That the bee, swimming in a pool of pebbles,
On it's last legs as such
And breathing forth its heart and soul
Was stuff.

That a cornucopia of leaves
In shades and tones and hues
Of lobster, cinnamon, cerise, vermillion
And beige is, in effect, the stuff.

On the question of significance of stuff
I further testify that the four
Young mice in the oneness of an Autumnal
Host and hoard of golden stubble was life.

The court may well deliberate how much
Is deemed sufficient as to tip the scales
Might I suggest and draw attention to the fact
That stuff is in the eye of the beholder
And very much a question for the heart
As the snowdrop said to the shy crocus.

Brendan Connolly

The Talking Lions Of Africa
(For Ronan, aged 3)

You and I will go one promised day
To the golden plains of Africa
To stalk the talking lions there
Some day soon when we have no cares

You and I will go one promised day
To the snowy tracts of Antarctica
To hear the talking penguins there
One day soon when we have no cares

You and I will go one promised day
To the crimson sands of Australia
To glimpse the talking jackaroos there
Perhaps one day when we have no cares

There are no lions, birds or bears that speak
Nor a time I imagine when I'll have no care
But because you imagine a place that is so
Just close your eyes and you'll be there.

Mary Matthews

The Thoroughfares Of My Town

The thoroughfares of my town
Are blessed by quiet reason,
A slow, deep webbing
Cast through cold centuries of doubt.

The children that play here,
Waiting to become
The sudden line in the breach
Shaping the unset stones,
Filling adult voices with a new song.

Brian Eardley

The Tides of Home

With weary tread I climb the mountain way,
My restless heart still yearning for the dunes.
The heritage of salt spray in my blood
Calls ever to the ocean's mirrored moons.

They cannot know who tramp the trackless sands,
The brooding pain that will not set me free
I would behold the tide sweep in once more
With secrets of the deep borne ruthlessly:

A ragged scarf that was a woman's joy;
A painted toy clasped in a baby's hand;
An orange wreath which once adorned a bride,
A violin that drifts towards the sand;

A wreath of sea-weed, like a laurel-crown,
Close clinging to a sailor's raven head;
The whispering of fisher folk at dawn
Who prayerfully kneel down and claim their dead.

This mountain path that leads beyond the clouds
May mark my footprint 'til the day I die
But in my heart the tides of home will flow
And in my ears will sound the sea gull's cry.

Adrian Saich

The Times of Oppression and Hunger

Yes, the winter is past, for all of us,
But the summer days will never be the same again.
Not after the loss of the innocence we once had.

My dear, I can still see you with your huge soulful eyes
Staring hurt and scared into the darkness of the woods
Where the men waited, wanting to annihilate
Everything that was sacred to your people.
You were so thin and weak, I dreamed you were dying.
I lifted you in my arms, and tried to hold you still.
I cried with the people of sorrows for thousands of
years.
The weeping that would never cease spiralling
Into the universe of sorrow. And joy,
And sorrow. And the weeping went on and on
Until we thought that sorrow would never come to an
end.

My love, if we would only try to make amends.
Maybe the furtive running back, looking for the boy.
Crying his name out in the dark.
Then maybe our souls might go on fire,
And we would try again and again
'Til the children would sleep in comfort,
And peace would settle.
And with Jesus we might call out for the eternal
Goodness.
Then maybe in the morning the sun would rise, as it
always had.

Bríd McDonnell

Though I be Mute

If I should mute my voice tonight
And never speak of love again
If I should wrap a silken shroud
About my heart's unuttered pain
What need if I must one day walk
Along the city's crowded street
And by good fortune or by bad
You are the one I chance to meet?
Though I am mute the gleam of love
Articulate through all disguises
Would pierce a million hidden tears
And smile at you from out my eyes.

Adrian Saich

Thoughts

How does it happen
What goes on
One day they're with you,
The next they're gone?
You're told what will happen
What to expect
But you go on hoping
And remain perplexed.

Cancer that dreadful word
The one you wish you had never heard
It's cruel and vile and has no discrimination
Of age or sex or even religion.
It's sly and hides and hangs around
Silent, crafty, not easily found.

I hope one day someone will find
An absolute cure for the whole of mankind.
Then no-one will ever have to see
The demise of beloved people
It took from me.

Pauline Mendoza

To A Tree

It's true
you can see God
in a tree
through your inner eye.

When you agree
with the heart
and understand
the creator's art.

It's true
when it's let be
this leafy radiance
grows in you and me.

Out of the blue
wonders fly in
to the drama of a day
making it new.

It's true
what matters
is peace and harmony
divinely truthful in a tree.

Thomas Clarke

Tobar An Tsolais, Killineer
(For Anne-Marie)

When the well
of light
is bloodied,
and the way lost,
I want to be
like that ash;
at midnight
to uproot myself,
and lead my life
elsewhere

But when words
well up in me
like tears,
I'll know
I have found
my way.

Susan Connolly

Tomorrow

The rain in the wind I feel its chill.
Storm clouds gathering I ponder God's will
The waters are rising, global warming they say
Nobody bothers about the next day.
Flooding and hurricanes here now to stay
Summer and winter when will we pay?
I walk on the sands and think of these things
Will anyone care if no bird sings?

Daphne Vernon

Tormenting Shadows of the Mind

Be still racing thoughts
Quiet my mind
Peace and silence
I pray
Replace with thoughts of
Dreaming sunbeams
Spider webs on frosted mornings
A summer's evening's sunset
In Haggardstown
A verse of a good song
To jam along to
The hope of a new start.

Rose Denner

Touch

I love the touch of my teddy; my teddy feels
Smooth, cosy and warm.
I like the touch of my baby nephew's skin;
It feels soft, cuddly and smooth
I like the touch of my mum's cuddles;
They feel warm and safe.
I like the touch of my clothes;
They are soft and comfortable.
I like the touch of my fluffy pencil case;
It is soft and furry.
I could touch them all day.

Siobhan McCartney

Trapped

When the wind is calm,
And the ocean mild
All I see in your eyes
Is the face of a child.

A frown on her face,
She cannot breathe air.
There are millions of spiders
Entwining her hair.

I start to get worried,
She cannot get out
"Release her, release her,"
I begin to shout.

She can't leave,
For you don't hear me
You fear me,
So she's trapped.

Inside a mind
That is controlled,
By thoughtless fears,
And tears of gold.

The tears of gold
That I can see,
Are not in you,
But within me.

I can't quite comprehend,
Why this girl is my friend.
For she's inside your mind,
Am I really that blind?

There is fear all around her,

I see it all in your eyes.
You are frightening her, hurting her,
Please stop, she will die.

It has all become clear now,
I can finally feel free.
For the girl that I see in you,
Is just a reflection of me!

Christine Mullaney

Triptych

Rock, wind, the desired one is on the strand.
I remembered climbing the sacred air,
The plunging sea -
Of an old time in a museum, futhering.
Youth was exceptionally happy.
I can't climb the stairs.
Help me. But the now is in waiting for resurrection.
All my dreams are wading on the periphery,
Waiting for the hill-walking
To inspire my nervous pump.
Shell of the ancient triptych
Of birth, death and hereafter.

Bríd McDonnell

Underground

Running down the metal escalator steps
To find both our trains at standstill, a
Quick hug before going our separate ways,
Rushing to lie back on cloth blue seats, and
Listen to underground's evening grumble.

Window reflections, bouncing off in every
Direction, a time to unfold a newspaper or
Look down at shoes, avoiding the eye of
People with white-knuckle grip of handrails.

Feeling the maniacal grind, pushing
Once more into light, sudden stop at each
Station, opening doors to breathe out and
Inhale new people.

Getting home with this shadowy space we
Create, sharing seats with strangers to get
Where we want to go, with a jostling sense
Of confused satisfaction surging through
Us all.

John Noonan

Until The End of Time

The old man sits in his cottage
That once was a joyful home
But tonight his heart is broken
For he sits there all alone

The tears in his eyes from weeping
They flow down his furrowed cheeks
And the strain from lack of sleeping
Has his body sore and weak

He holds in his hands a picture
With age it's battered and torn
It's the wedding picture of himself and Mary
The wife he must now mourn

Their life together was happy
Though children they had none
But the Lord blessed them in other ways
And together they were as one

Slowly the night goes on
And his eyes they start to close
And a vision comes before him
Of a place where everything glows

He dreams he is in heaven
Walking among angels fair
And he sees his darling Mary
With her long and golden hair

She beckons him to join her
With a warm and peaceful smile
And they stroll together through paradise
Their hearts for ever entwined

Then suddenly he is awoken
And his face has a lamentful stare

He looks around for Mary
But tonight she is not there

Like flotsam on the tide of life
Or a dead tree's withered leaf
He is a lost soul in a lonely world
With no one to share his grief

The teardrops are in his eyes
And till death they will stay
Until the angels come to call for him
On his final day

Till then he will go on grieving
And drink his glass of bitter wine
But Mary will always be in his heart
Until the end of time.

Patrick Furey

Valentine's Day Present To A Friend

I fell in love again today
She was quietly searching the government documents
Archived in the library
I could smell her sweet dark hair
And feel the softness of her olive skin
On my coarse fingers.
I imagined our love affair,
Gentle yet passionate.
We would calm each other
While stirring the fire,
An unquenchable thirst for one another,
Until, having each absorbed the other totally,
We would be as one.

She was gone in five minutes,
Normal service resumed.
You and I are kindred spirits
In our unrequited loves and unrestrained dreams.
This is the way of the romantic fool.
If the fool is the wisest of all
Let me use myself as an example -
The result of wasting energy
On fantasy, not action.
And if I took action, what then?
Happiness?

What am I supposed to write with that?

The pen is the lover
Of all who have yet to learn.

Conor Duffy

Waif

Childless ones whose eyes are kind,
Take him quick and let him find
All of love that he has missed!
Little rose-like face unkissed -
Let it press against your lips.
Kiss his fragile finger tips!
Such a tiny helpless form!
Let his nestling body bless
Arms that ache with emptiness.

Adrian Saich

Walk

They pass me by, the endless rows
Firmly rooted, natures best
Ready to march, all follow suit

This endless quest, to surface once more
Cut through the roots that bind

Memories flood back
Drystone walls, hedgerows
Cascading waterfalls tumble by
A gate of sorts I reach, friendly dog in view

God's palette in rust, timeless and strong
Strange locking mechanism, still works though
Nature tries it's best to restrict, to hold back
Laid out like a minefield, open to view, the mire
                                        below
But somehow I survive

Still, they pass by row by row
Rooted strongly they dance and shake
Happy with nature's haunting melody

I reach a churchyard, gates wide open
In wait for God's audience perhaps?
A timeless question it seems, who knows?
God perhaps!

Just keeps going round

Still, nice walk of sorts.

Simon Scott

Walk With The Tide

What mighty hand holds back
These roaring beasts?
Surging relentlessly
Grasping for land
Once calm beneath their claws

What mighty hand holds up?
These thirsty cliffs
Leaning to hear their roar
But never bending
To drink their foamy waves?

Walk the beach and wonder
With the tide that comes and goes
Enjoy the sunshine
Salty air
And the sand between your toes.

Adrian Saich

Waste

Plunder finite resources
Trees, soil, air, water systems
Consumerist refined senses
Unwrap glossy packaging
In its multiple layers

Bury and burn the evidence
And push it out of sight
It has to go somewhere
Arrogantly stated
And then subject our neighbours
To rotting decomposing poisoned smells

This greenhouse, my new dysfunctional abode
Where oxygen is replaced with carbon dioxide
A leaking roof, its ozone disappearing
It's culture! Chorofluoracarbons, nitrous oxides
Ultraviolet radiation
Our friends, nature's species are baling out.

Bernadette Martin

Water

Fresh and cool
At birth and death
And in between
Enriches you

Sluggish in attire
Demeanour discoloured
Rheumatoid reflexes
As it winds a weary passage
Through grimy recesses

Bottled water has replaced
The bloom of bygone days
Shopping trolleys full of it
Corporate profits rise

O Creator!
Did you plan
A surcharge for your goods
This middleman
A giant with golden claws
And silken jaws
Cares not.

Bernadette Martin

Weeding

Smell the warm moist clay
It will yield the nasty weeds
Without a struggle

Chickweed must come out
Your descendants are many
If you get a chance

Scotch grass, what a scourge
You travel far and quickly
Underneath the soil

Speedwell, pretty bloom
I like your cute little blue face
But you too must go

Ouch! Cursed nettle
Lurking under the dahlia
Like a cunning asp

I must find a dock
To counteract your venom
And relieve my pain.

Maureen Kerrigan

Well Fever

Toberboice, Tobereisk,
Tober na Caillí.
Saint Brigid's Well,
Dunleer -
lost, found
and lost again.
Saint Mairéad's Well,
Toberdoney -
a babbling well.
Garrett's Well, Hacklim;
Garrett's well of the
setting sun

Tober Sí, Gallstown -
the 'fairy well'.
Spa Well, Marley -
a well that takes care
of itself.
Tober Mháire, Mullary:
dedicated to Mary -
a spring fragile
in old age.
The well at Listoke -
some call it
the well at Ballymakenny

Shanlis, Hacklim, Cappoge,
Kildemock, Carnanbreaga -
townland names
dancing to the sound
of their own word-music.
Toberfinn, Tobertheorin,
Toberhullamog.
And three more yet
to find -
Tober mín, Tober Chomhaill,
Tober na gCorr,

'well of the herons'...

Let every step
bring me closer.
I want to taste
your stillness.
An ash tree
is a signpost
to you,
a roadside stile
your threshold.
Motorists
zoom past you
unaware.
I sense
your different
guises.
Always the same
surprise
as I find you,
touch your water
that lets me
see further,
the other
deeper side
of here.

Susan Connolly

Wilting Shades

Blessed is thee,
encroached within the Wealth of Nations.
Profiteering righteously with that prosperous
soul.
Holes and miles make up our roads,
they dug doggedly, digging further
down further clapping
carelessly on ill silhouettes that
hung forever, sick thoughts
of collapse haunt the hunting's
of grey grey grabbling wolves.
Surrounded surreptitiously, skulking shots
Of gold down our throats 'til
drunken drools of ecstatic's reap
With good cause, true people,
gifted and corrupt retreated back near
heavenly skies, resting relentlessly on
murky mountains maintaining the
crooked realism of what would come.
Come come now, shame and blame
retain our human maim,
forcing poor us to leave homes,
goods we possess rise and
live within our new entrenched souls.
Wombs of all men pillage the
last remaining good infant.
Poor child who smiles and dies
is happiest.
We no longer cry but in our
pain, eat, eat the devouring
rage 'til it fills us, rays of rape
shoot out our eyes and the rose
of life wilts slowly, surely dying
in a sepulchral state of wisdom.
Roots, uprooted and eaten by our vile,
in her absence all we feel is the pain.

Adrian Neasy

Winter

(Extract from a recovered diary...
Sunday, 7th November 2004.)

A dark bird flew into the sun, pink,
silhouette tripping the tongue,
haunting.
Ethereal November light spilt across the world,
liquid as from a cool decanter.
November, like an ultraviolet flower.

The leaves were brushed to the roadside,
swept away autumn.

The pictures by the lake were everywhere.

A mist clung to her, seeping silver.

Ethereal November light spilt across the world.

They called her *Winter.*

I thought she was pretty as a flower, not alien.

Orla Fay

Winter Sonnet

It has been freezing hard all night
Land, river and pond are frozen
Icicles hang long, strong and bright
As the sun shines cool and brazen

Through the elastic atmosphere
Come voices of children sliding
On a frozen pond, without fear.
Of danger they have no inkling

A blackbird flies from yonder bush
Laughing as he passes the gate
He startles the elegant thrush
And robin sings out to his mate

The frozen stillness is broken
But the magic is unspoken.

Maureen Kerrigan

World Wide

Men, continue to die
To lie, in a special place
Beneath
The shade of trees
Remembered, with honour.

While peace signs a lease
For the light of night
The dark of day
And, a man eats crumbs
From a silver tray.

Not seeing
The doom and gloom
As a god of war

Leaves beside him
A broken wreath.

Laura Bruce

Worthwhile

These things make life worthwhile
The flashing of jewel on work-worn hands,
The patter of rain on parching lands,
A ray of sunlight 'cross my book
The gleam of firelight in our hearthside nook,
And from a new-made friend a smile.

Adrian Saich

You That Know Who You Are

Wrap me in a blanket
Made of pieces of the past
Let me study the stitching
And patchwork of my life

Take me away with you
So I won't go insane
And I will take with me
Only my blanket

Nothing could mean more to me
Than you and my memories
So let's lie and live forever
Covered in my life.

Caroline McEvoy

Your Little Angel

I watched as the mourners filed into the house,
Unaware of the pain our family were in,
Put on a brave face my mother would say,
I've never seen her look so fragile, so thin.

I watched as my dad cried silently,
I'd never seen him cry much at all.
It was amazing to me, how a grown man his age,
Could look so tired, so small.

My brother and sisters stayed up in their rooms,
Expressing their grief and sorrows.
For me, however, tears could not come,
Every minute seemed like hours.

The doctors informed us she was seriously ill,
Good chance of her getting better, she was young,
But here we where holding her funeral,
Looks like the doctors where wrong.

I grabbed hold of her diary
Beside her bed,
Opened it to the last entry,
My heart filled with dread.

In the last entry,
What it read,
I'll tell you now,
As I lie on her bed.

Dear family and friends, I know you are sad,
But please dry those tears, mum and dad.
I know that this may feel like treason,
But I was put here for a reason.
I was made from kindness and love,
As I was sent from God above,
You might not believe me but I hope you do,

Because what I have said is true.
I've spent fifteen wonderful years with you,
But I have to move on, and you should too.
I have to spread joy to others now,
So please cheer up if you can somehow.
I love you so much, I hope you remember,
That you took care of Gods little helper.
I know that you had called me Rachael,
But please remember me as your little Angel.

Sarah Crosby

INDEX OF POEMS

Index of Poems
...by Author

259

261

ISBN 141207601-3